I dedicate this book to God, without whom I wouldn't be who I am today.

PURIFY YOUR LIFE

AMANDA GUISEPPI

PURIFY YOUR LIFE

Copyright © 2018 Amanda Guiseppi

All rights reserved.

ISBN: 9781729310861

Cover image by Canva.com

TABLE OF CONTENTS

INTRODUCTION: WHAT IS PURITY? 1

PROLOGUE 4

CHAPTER 1: PURITY IN FINANCES 6

CHAPTER 2: PURITY IN EMOTIONS 19

CHAPTER 3: PURITY IN RELATIONSHIPS 37

CHAPTER 4: PURITY IN MIND 52

CHAPTER 5: PURITY IN WAITING 68

CHAPTER 6: PURITY IN LEADERSHIP 85

CONCLUSION 92

EPILOGUE 96

APPENDIX A 100

APPENDIX B 101

RESOURCES 102

REFERENCES 103

INTRODUCTION: WHAT IS PURITY?

Striving to live a life of purity in a world of darkness.

"Because one person disobeyed God, many became sinners." (Romans 5:19, NLT) One the results of the sin of Adam is that we all ended up being/will be born in sin. So today, my question is, in a world that is so corrupt and filled with wickedness how do we as Christians maintain the purity that has been given to us through the Holy Spirit?

I knew that there were already a ton of books written on the subject of purity; sexual purity to be exact. So, I prayed and asked God what exactly He wanted me to write about as there was already a lot that had been written on the subject. Then I felt challenged to define purity in regards to my own experience and according to biblical standards.

In order for us to truly understand purity, let's look at its biblical definition. The New Bible Dictionary defines purity as "ceremonial." "It (purity) was to be obtained by certain ablutions and purifications which were enjoined upon the worshipper in the performance of his religious duties."[i] However, in the New Testament after Jesus sent the Holy Spirit down to earth, there was a shift in purifying the physical to a purification of the spiritual and moral (heart).[ii] Jesus talks about this in Mark 7: *"'It's not what goes into your body that defiles you; you are defiled by what comes from your heart." 20 And then he added, "It is what comes from inside that defiles you. 21 For from within, out of a person's heart, come evil thoughts, sexual immorality, theft, murder, 22 adultery, greed, wickedness, deceit, lustful desires, envy, slander, pride, and foolishness. [23] All these vile things come from within; they are what defile you.'"* (Mark 7: 19-23, NLT) So purity in New Testament biblical terms is a heart issue; it's about stripping away the dirt and filth that Jesus talks about in our hearts.

To take this one step further, let's see how the dictionary defines purity: "Freedom from adulteration or contamination." It goes on to say "freedom from immorality, especially of a sexual nature."[iii] So the dictionary defines purity as the accomplished task of freeing oneself of impurity.

In light of the biblical and dictionary definitions, and for the purposes of this book, I define purity as: the process of removing impurity (in thoughts, words and actions) from your life. The great apostle Paul explains this process very clearly. He explains how we are to live in purity in every area of our lives:

[13] For you have been called to live in freedom, my brothers and sisters. But don't use your freedom to satisfy your sinful nature. Instead, use your freedom to serve one another in love. [14] For the whole law can be summed up in this one command: "Love your neighbor as yourself.[15] But if you are always biting and devouring one another, watch out! Beware of destroying one another.

Living by the Spirit's Power

[16] So I say, let the Holy Spirit guide your lives. Then you won't be doing what your sinful nature craves. [17] The sinful nature wants to do evil, which is just the opposite of what the Spirit wants. And the Spirit gives us desires that are the opposite of what the sinful nature desires. These two forces are constantly fighting each other, so you are not free to carry out your good intentions. [18] But when you are directed by the Spirit, you are not under obligation to the law of Moses.

[19] When you follow the desires of your sinful nature, the results are very clear: sexual immorality, impurity, lustful pleasures, [20] idolatry, sorcery, hostility, quarreling, jealousy, outbursts of anger, selfish ambition, dissension, division, [21] envy, drunkenness, wild parties, and other sins like these. Let me tell you again, as I have before, that anyone living that sort of life will not inherit the Kingdom of God.

²² But the Holy Spirit produces this kind of fruit in our lives: love, joy, peace, patience, kindness, goodness, faithfulness, ²³ gentleness, and self-control. There is no law against these things!
²⁴ Those who belong to Christ Jesus have nailed the passions and desires of their sinful nature to his cross and crucified them there. ²⁵ Since we are living by the Spirit, let us follow the Spirit's leading in every part of our lives. ²⁶ Let us not become conceited, or provoke one another, or be jealous of one another.
Galatians 5:13-26 (NLT- emphasis added)

So how do we do that? How do we strip away all the impurity from our lives? What does that look like?

When I was first challenged to write a book about purity I had just finished an eleven-month intensive program called, Single to Married God's Way, No More GAGA (GAGA back then). (Check out this great reference in my list of resources at the end of the book) This program focused on working on myself to become the right person before God brought the right person into my life (my future husband). One of its main focuses was on purification, so this concept was not foreign to me. What I was not prepared for was how God was going to weave this notion of purity into every area of my life over the next few years. Slowly, but surely God has been showing me how to live a life of purity in my finances, relationships, my mindset, in my circumstances like promotion, in my seasons of waiting and even through my emotions. God showed me that my thoughts, words and actions were not lining up with his word, which is pure. So, something had to change.

It is my hope that through this book you can begin to rid your life of the impurity that is holding you back from fulfilling the purpose of why you have been put on this earth. 2 Timothy 2:21 states *"If you keep yourself pure, you will be a special utensil for honorable use. Your life will be clean, and you will be ready for the Master to use you for every good work."* (NLT) My prayer is that YOU, reading this book right now, through the lessons of this book, will be ready to be used by God "for every good work."

PROLOGUE

There was a time when I had to have a difficult conversation with a friend. I went into this particular conversation thinking we were going to discuss the past weekend's events. A few incidents transpired over the weekend so I was adamant that I wanted to discuss them with her and thought she felt the same way. Instead, what transpired was that a list of my faults and mistakes were brought to light and no discussion about the weekend was even mentioned. A piece of paper was taken out with a list of the all the things I was/wasn't doing: wrong attitudes that I had, mistakes I had made, etc. I had to sit there and listen to this list of my dirty laundry being aired out right in front of my face.

I was shocked and stunned and could not say a word. I just sat there in disbelief and listened, and then I inevitably started to cry. (A side note: I struggle with talking about myself to others, let alone talking about my faults.) I felt like I was being forced to face parts of me that I did not want to look at. With that said, talking about my faults with others was an area that I was trying to be better at; I would ask my friends to be completely honest with me when they felt I was getting out of line or if I was overstepping boundaries. Let's be clear that this was not the case here; I did not give this person permission to speak into my life. But, when all was said and done there was truth to what she was saying although the delivery was not the best. So yes, she could have delivered it better, but the fact was she didn't, so now I was faced with a choice.

In instances such as these we have a choice to either learn from them and grow or to ignore them and become non-trusting and bitter. In my case, I ignored it at first, but those faults started coming out in other ways down the road. So, we either deal with those parts of ourselves we find "ugly" sooner, or later. Either way we will have to deal with them eventually. This is all part of the process of purification that God puts each and every one of us through.

David talks about this process in Psalm 66 where he states *"You have tested us, O God; you have purified us like silver. You captured us in your net and laid the burden of slavery on our backs. Then you put a leader over us. We went through fire and flood, but you brought us to a place of great abundance."* (Psalm 66:10-12, NLT) God tests us. Like the Israelites, He allows us to go through tragedies, hardships and troubles. Similar to that of my example earlier, God allowed the hard truth to be told to me in that manner, because He knew I needed to hear it. Not only that, but I believe God wanted me to learn from the experience, therefore refining or purifying my character. God's promise after we go through the process is that He will bring us to a place of great abundance. Another version states that He will bring us to *"a safe place."* (Psalm 66:12, ESV) Yet another version states that *"He has brought us out to freedom!"* (Psalm 66:12, CEB) God wants us to be free from our old selves, that self that was knee deep in sin and darkness, that self that was drenched in disobedience. Not because we knew better, but because we didn't know better.

Hebrews 12:1 talks about this purification process:

"... let us strip off every weight that slows us down, especially the sin that so easily trips us up. And let us run with endurance the race God has set before us." (NLT)

The writer talks about a process of stripping off. The original Greek word for strip off in this verse is *apotithémi* which comes from the Greek words: *apo* and *tithémi*. *Apo* means from or away from. *Tithémi* means to place or lay. So together *apotithémi* means to lay aside, or put away.[iv] The writer of Hebrews is calling us to take those sins that easily trip us up (fear, doubt, anger, etc.) and lay it aside from us. So, if you struggle with anxious thoughts, put them out of your mind as soon as they come in- lay them aside out of your mind. I know this is easier said than done, but it's all part of the process and it will take time for us to be victorious.

Now that we know, we can have hope in God whenever we go through this process, that He is taking us to a better place, a better version of ourselves.

CHAPTER 1: PURITY IN FINANCES

I have to admit that when I started to explore this topic of purity, finances was not the first category that came to mind. Purity in finances simply means managing the money that God has given you on this earth in purity. What does this look like? Well God has called us to be good stewards of His money. That means saving, being generous, tithing and learning to trust God with all of it.

At the age of 24 my Aunt passed away from cancer. She was like a second mother to me. We were so similar in personality and she just understood me. Her death started me on a trajectory to find myself. That path led me straight to London, England. Instead of finding myself there I ended up finding something much more precious: Jesus. And it was through Jesus that I found my true self.

Before I came to faith, I was a big spender. I even remember spending £1000 just on clothes during a holiday in Greece. As soon as I would make money, I would spend it. I even received a £5000 loan from the bank to support my spending habit. Plus, I had £1500 worth of credit cards and a £1000 overdraft limit. You see the thing with spending money that isn't yours is that you have to pay it back. I was in an apartment that cost me over half of my income just for living expenses. I had to get a second job just to keep up with my lavish lifestyle.

Shortly after I came to faith, I quit my job and through a series of events I found myself back home in Canada living with my parents again! So here I was living in my parents' house and looking for a job. At that time all I had to my name was CAD$100 that I had received from my godmother at Christmas the year before when I came home for a visit. I remember wanting to hold onto that money for as long as possible as I didn't have a job yet and didn't know if more was coming my way anytime soon. My move really showed me how I truly handled money. It highlighted my financial impurity; selfish and lavish spending, not saving, incurring debt, etc.

After I came home I learned my first true lesson about money: God is our provider. I was used to spending everything I had and the only things I would save up for were trips and shopping sprees, but now I had to really put my hope in God and wait patiently for His provision. (Romans 8:25) I had to learn to trust God that He was my provider. Since I quit my job in London, until I moved back in with my parents, God took me through a process of stripping away. What God did was remove the item that I was misusing to show me what I was doing wrong, to emphasize my impurity.

Just over a month after I had returned home, God blessed me with a job at St. Joseph's hospital. The hospital is not an easy place to get your foot in the door so this was truly a God thing. It was part time, but it paid very well. And before I got my first paycheck, I was able to purchase bus tickets to get myself to and from work and pay for the occasional lunch with the $100 I had. I made the decision not to spend that money right away as soon as I got home. I believe that one decision of waiting to spend the money allowed me enjoy it even more later on than if I had spent it right away.

David speaks about those who wait on the Lord in Psalm 27:14: *"Wait for the Lord; Be strong and let your heart take courage; Yes, wait for the Lord."* When I waited on God's timing to spend that money, I thoroughly enjoyed it. It was God's way of providing transportation for my new job plus extra blessing of being able to buy my lunch. When we wait on God, we will never be disappointed. The principle I learned here was saving. I learned that when we put off spending our money right away, we reap benefits (paying for an unexpected expense, blessing someone else, buying something for yourself, meeting a need, etc.). When we delay instant gratification of saving up and waiting to spend money, we learn to wait on God and get to see how He works things out for our good. How are you at saving? Do you save a part of each pay cheque? Have you started saving for your future? It's never too early or too late to start saving.

~~~

I was working at my job at the hospital and things were going well, although it was a temporary job which they kept extending the contract month by month; I was really hoping for something more permanent. That time finally came in September of that year. I applied for and got a job at another hospital, a one-year contract, with benefits and a much higher pay. I was so excited and grateful.

I remember praying right after the interview for the job and saying to God "if you give me this job I will start tithing from the first pay cheque I receive." Now remember I had newly come to faith so the concept of tithing was not even on my radar. I grew up Catholic so I believed in giving offering as in the you-give-what-you-can principle. Let me say that there is nothing wrong with that mentality, but now I can confidently say that I live by what the word of God says. In Malachi 3:10, it states: *"Bring the full tithe into the storehouse, that there may be food in my house. And thereby put me to the test, says the LORD of hosts, if I will not open the windows of heaven for you and pour down for you a blessing until there is no more need."* (ESV) Through the prophet Malachi, God was convicting His church that they need to bring the tithes into the storehouse. Today the storehouse is the church. God wants us to tithe, it was always His plan. And His promise is that he will "open the windows of heaven and pour out a blessing until there is no more need." I don't know about you, but I want God's blessing in my life so I obeyed His Word.

You see at that point I wasn't tithing- I was just giving an offering, an amount of money that I felt like giving. For those of you unfamiliar with the concept of tithing: it is giving the first 10% of our income back to God. Basically, God is asking that when we get money (whether that's a pay cheque, payment for services, etc.) that we give 10% of it to His church (ultimately back to Him). For some of you this may be a really hard concept to digest. What helped me when I was first learning about tithing was that I had gone from making no money to making quite a bit of money. So, if God was asking me to give away what I didn't have in the first place (started off with much less), it was an easy decision. That was my situation, but everyone's story is different. You may not have gotten that raise and are barely making ends meet now. I don't know how God does it, but He challenges us to trust him by giving 10% of our money back to him. His promise is that He will open up the windows of heaven and pour out a blessing. (Malachi 3:10) How we tithe is different for everyone. Some may say they tithe on their net income, some on their gross income, some tithe on every bit of money that comes their way including gifts. That part is between you and God. But when you get to a place where you love God more than money, than tithing is just your way of showing him how much you love him as you obey His Word. This is how we are good stewards of what He has blessed us with here on earth and how we live out purity in our finances.

When I got the job, I started to tithe immediately. On top of that, and I believe this was God, I felt strongly that I needed to get myself out of debt- I didn't want it in my life anymore. Plus, I didn't really like owing people money. So, I started with the smallest debt first in the UK. Later, I learned this was a good thing to do according to Dave Ramsey, a Financial Expert. I was doing what he coined as the "debt snowball" -- starting with the smallest debt and working my way up to the largest. The concept works on wins, once you pay off smaller amounts you are motivated to pay off larger amounts.[v]

Remember my credit cards? Just a side note on this, the British pound was still doing very good at this point so anything I paid off would have to be exchanged into Canadian money, which back then was still double. So, my total debt of just over £7,000 was going to cost me at least CAD$15,000 to pay off, and this was on top of the debt I had accrued from being an international student in the UK. I planned to pay off my debt by allotting half of each pay cheque, after tithes, towards my debt. That started in October 2011, and by March 2012 I had paid off <u>all</u> my debt in the UK- $15,000 of it. So, I continued to pay off my Canadian debt (line of credit and student loans), starting with the smaller one. By August 2012- in just 11 months- I had paid off half of my total debt combined of $50,000, that included all my debt in the UK, plus my small Canadian debt- I still had the big debt to pay off. I don't know about you but that just blows my mind! And being the brand spanking new Christian I was at the time; my faith was built. It showed me that when God puts something in your heart and He is behind you, that nothing will stop you from achieving that thing.

It also showed me that when you pour into the Kingdom and give God what belongs to God, that He will bless you. God's Word promises us that when we bring the whole tithe (Malachi 3:10) into His Temple (church) that he will bless us. That's what God did for me- He provided me a job with better pay so that He could bless me with extra money so I could pay off my debts. That moment increased my faith in God when it came to finances and solidified my decision to continue to tithe no matter what. Step by step God was teaching me how to live out purity in finances, by first saving, and then tithing and then paying off my debts. I was well on my way to removing all impure habits where money was concerned.

In and about the time I was aggressively paying off my debt, my church was doing a building fund and asking for pledges as we were preparing to build a second campus. I prayed about it and felt God challenge me to give a certain amount.

I was a little hesitant paying off my debt and paying rent to my parents, on how I was going to make these payments. That's when I decided to take matters into my own hands. I took the amount that God put in my heart and tried to establish my own steps in terms of the payment in the name of "faith." Instead of trusting God to provide for me, I made a choice to take away half the money I was giving my parents for rent and put it into the building fund. Well that didn't go over well with my parents and therein started a long battle that could have been avoided from the beginning.

I didn't know that once you make a pledge, then you leave it up to God to provide what goes beyond what you can give. That is where the true faith part came into play. Instead, I made plan to try and come up with the money on my own. And that is simply not how it works.

Months later, in frustration and confusion as to why God told me to give so much, (it caused distress in my home and my spirit) I humbled myself and asked Him to show me what I was missing. This was the Scripture that He gave me: *"But those who won't care for their relatives, especially those in their own household, have denied the true faith. Such people are worse than unbelievers"* (1 Timothy 5:8). He revealed to me that His intention was never for me to stop paying money towards my parents, but He wanted me to trust in him to come through with what I didn't have each month. It was too late for me make it right when I realized this, but I learned. And I apologized to my parents for this. Over the next few months I made monthly payments towards my building fund and ended up paying it off a month early through the use of my tax return that year.

It was the winter of 2011 and I was listening to the testimonies of the interns in our church who just came back from South Africa. I remember thinking that I wanted to go to South Africa. The opportunity finally came in the fall of 2012 for me to go Cape Town, South Africa, my first ever missions' trip. Well with the building pledge and me paying rent to my parents and making the minimum payments on my biggest debt, I couldn't really afford to save $2,785 plus spending money for a missions' trip. But I really wanted to go as I have always wanted to travel the world and what a better way to travel then by doing so for the Kingdom, right? Also, I prayed about it and I felt like I had confirmation to go on this trip (Side note: confirmation from God can take on so many forms. My suggestion would be to make sure your decision- what you think/know you heard God say to you- always lines up with God's word. A great way to do that is when praying about a decision, ask God to give you a Scripture that you can hold on to once the decision is made.)

So, I did what anyone who didn't have the money to go on a missions' trip would do: I fundraised. I was going to go as part of our church's dance team so the team got together to do a couple car washes to help with the costs. I also asked people I worked with to give to my trip. I sold homemade cupcakes and asked family members to support me financially. I remember it like it was yesterday- I received a call two weeks before the trip, being $200 short, from our Pastor and she had told me from the car washes we did together as a dance team that I had $200 to put towards my trip. That meant all $2785 was paid off. That was the first of other trips that God provided funding for me. My faith was stretched and grew quite a bit that day. I believe that this was in direct correlation to my faithfulness in tithing. Remember Malachi 3:10? I did my part and God was now doing His. I was reaping the benefits of living out purity in my finances.

Those who were sharing about the South African missions' trip were a mix of students doing the internship at our church and other members of our church. I really wanted to do the internship and felt called to do so. The internship was an unpaid time of taking Bible classes and volunteering within various departments of the church. It was also for "youth" and I wasn't quite that young. I was in my early adulthood at the time, but I knew I wanted to be a part, and a year later I was. However, in order to do the internship, we had to pay for it and the cost was $5000 for the year. God had just provided for my missions' trip so my faith was stirred to believe that He would come up with the money for this internship. Not only did God come through with funds for my internship, but He also gave me favour with my boss at the time to allow me to go down to part time. People don't really talk about the benefits of tithing, because if we did everybody would be tithing with the wrong intentions. We tithe because God says so and because we get to be a part of building His kingdom through giving to the church. Through my tax return I was able to pay off both building pledge a year earlier and the first year of my internship.

Fast forward one year later, the internship had finished and so was my work contract (remember the new better paying job that I got?). I found myself unemployed and on the hunt for another job, but not too long after I was offered a job at the church. Now the job I had before had a competitive salary and it was in a prestigious university, so to say that I would have to take a pay cut working for the church, would be an understatement. I had to pray about this decision, because it was not an easy decision to make. I mean I was used to making a lot more money and wanted to move out of my parents' house. Philippians 4:6 states "Don't be anxious about things; instead, pray. *Pray about everything.* He longs to hear your requests, so talk to God about your needs and be thankful for what has come." (The Voice, my emphasis added) Take every decision to God, so that He can guide you in what to do. Especially when it comes to your finances, you want to make sure that you are stewarding the money God has entrusted to you well. Even if you know what to do, it's always good practice to just take it to him. God may be able to show you something you are missing in the process and show you what His will is for your life. Remember we are meant to model Jesus, not our will but His will be done. (Matthew 26:39)

So, I prayed and God gave me Luke 6:32: *"If you love only those who love you, why should you get credit for that? Even sinners love those who love them…"* (NLT) confirming that He wanted me to take the position at the church. The thing is that I really struggled with accepting the salary I was going to make at the church and had a hard time seeing how God was going to provide for me via this job. Basically, God was challenging me through the Word He gave me that I can take this job with a lower salary and no benefits, while working to better His Kingdom or I can choose to go for a higher paying job like that of the world and go my own way, which ultimately leads to a life of unfulfillment. God was trying to show me that money wasn't everything and that those other jobs would have never satisfied me the way this job does now. God was opening my eyes to the bigger picture, the Kingdom picture that he sees.

I took that job, and three months into it (now remember this was already stretching me on how I was going to live off of my new salary) I was told by my friend who rented her extra room to me that she would have to raise my rent in a couple months as hydro was going up as would her expenses. I just figured out how to live on what I was making and then I was told my rent was going to increase by $100 per month. I decided that the next day I would go to my employer and tell them my situation and find out if there was a way they could possibly increase my pay. Though they empathized with my situation, they weren't able to accept my request. I felt stuck. All I could do was cry. I was devastated. I mean just months ago I believed that I heard from God that He wanted me to take this job and now this happened. And with my tear-soaked cheeks I went to the only source I knew- God. I prayed and asked God, what am I going to do? Why did you do this to me? And these were the words I felt God give to reassure me: *"And my God will meet all your needs according to the riches of His glory in Christ Jesus."* (Philippians 4:19, NIVUK)

You see God's Word promises that He will supply all our needs, not just some, but all. So, I had no other choice but to believe in His Word and trust in him. Two weeks later my boss came up to me, and through a set of circumstances, ended up offering me a sizeable raise that not only allowed me to pay my new rent amount but I was also able to save more money.

I have now been working for my church for about five years. In that time, I have moved from place to place a whopping five times. Three of those times my rent increased significantly, I received two more sizeable financial promotions at work. Both stories are great testimonies to God's hand at work in my life and how He is our true provider. Jehovah Jireh is one of the names of God used in the Bible is Jehovah Jireh which literally translated means "God will provide." We see this in Genesis 22 when Abraham goes to sacrifice his son in obedience to God. Just as he is about to kill his son, God provides a ram caught in a thicket for him to sacrifice instead. After that moment, Abraham calls the place where he almost sacrificed his son, Jehovah Jireh after God provides an animal for him to sacrifice instead.

The second financial promotion came in 2015. It was in the spring and I was living with some family while I was waiting for my new apartment to become available. This new place was $150 more in rent, but it was all-inclusive, so I had worked out how I was going to pay my rent. Sure, it was going to be tight, but God had always come through before. That summer, I ended up receiving my second financial promotion from the church where I was able to comfortably pay my new rent, adjust my budget to allow some more room in my entertainment money and save some more money.

Since this was first time I was moving out on my own in Canada, I had to buy furniture and I needed it fast because I found a place to live and had a move in date, but no furniture. One day in March, I received a phone call from my mother telling me that someone from an investment company in the US had contacted her looking for me and that I needed to call them back. When I called, they told me that my Aunt who had passed away ten years ago had some investments that needed be cashed in, as her account was about to close. I had found out that she had left me a portion of the money. She lived in the US, so I had a cheque coming in the mail for over $5000 in US funds. Yes, I know what you're thinking, 2015 was good year for me! And now I had money to buy all new furniture. This was just another example of my obedience to God's word in tithing, giving, saving and being faithful. The Bible says that when we are obedient God will bless us. (Deuteronomy 28:1-2) This is just one of the many ways God blessed my purity in my finances.

Later that year I developed one of the best habits that we could do to become better stewards of our money: budgeting. I had always budgeted or else I would not have been able to afford to live in the places I have lived, but this was different. I discovered a man by the name of Dave Ramsey and started listening to his podcast- The Dave Ramsey Show. (I highly recommend it for anyone in debt and wanting to get out of it.) He talked about the envelope system and budgeting every penny you earn. So that's what I did, and through that I saw God's hand of provision over my life even clearer. Every month I had money, $30-$50, left over. That was extra money I could save, spend or give away. It was amazing and opened up a whole new world for me. Budgeting is telling your money where to go not allowing it dictate where you go. It's getting a vision each month of what you're going to do with your finances. (Proverbs 29:18)

A year later, through another series of events, I found myself needing a new place to live. So, a friend of mine from high school graciously opened up their home to allow me to stay with them for almost three months. Do you get it? God never left me and forsook me. (God makes that promise in the Bible five times: once from David to Solomon as he refers to the Scriptures, three times to Joshua and once to the modern-day Jews as a reminder. [1 Chronicles 28:20, Deuteronomy 31:6 & 8, Joshua 1:5, and Hebrews 13:5]) He is always right beside us ready to provide every step of the way.

This space was temporary to give me time to look for a permanent place where I would finally settle. I kind of had a thing for moving, I was almost like the Goldilocks of apartment living; I kept apartment-hunting until I found the one that was "just right." So, in October of that year I found the most perfect place, it was newly renovated, but there was one problem- it was way out of my budget. Insert the hand of God here where He would provide for me once again. I was up for a third promotion, but this time it was a new role where I would be taking on more responsibility and more hours. I was told that it would come with a financial promotion, but I wasn't sure when that promotion was coming and how much it would be. When I did find out how much it would be, it turned out that this place was affordable for me but was right at the top end of my budget. There would be no wiggle room. Normally I would say "No way, hosay!" because I liked having a bit of a buffer when it comes to balancing my living expenses compared to my income. I have always heard that your living expenses should not be more than 1/3 of your income. This was not the case with this apartment. But I decided that I would take a chance and see how God could come through for me financially. Since I started budgeting I was really good at staying within a budget and it trained me to be able to live on a very tight budget. I prayed about it and I decided to take the place. Since then I have had constant financial provision coming out of everywhere, God simply is/was/will be my provider.

WHAT I LEARNED

As I look back over the last six years, I am floored at how good God is to His children. There are three key lessons I learned in order to maintain purity in our finances:

Do everything to the Lord. *1 Corinthians 10:31 states "So whether you eat or drink, or whatever you do, do it all for the glory of God."* (NLT) What this meant for me is that every decision I made with my money should have the motive of bringing glory to God, not myself or man. There are three ways we can bring glory to God in our finances: stewarding, spending, and giving.

1. *Stewarding*: Steward means "to manage or look over (another's property)."[vi] One of the ways I steward the money I am given is when I budget. What I am doing is setting myself up so that God can use me to bless others. God only blesses us so that we can be a blessing to others.

2. *Spending*: We should always ask ourselves this question: When we spend money, are we doing it in a way that brings glory to God? If He were to question our motives for spending, would we be confident in our answers or ashamed?

   Some wrong thinking, we can get into with spending could be: to fill a void we are feeling that can only be filled by God; to soothe emotional wounds which we need to seek God heal. Don't get me wrong, there are probably many times we spend money for the right reasons: to buy something we need, to treat ourselves or because we just want to and there are no unhealthy emotions attached to that.

(Side note: treating oneself without being selfish or gluttonous can be a challenge. But the difference is your decision to treat yourself after a long work day or after a period of hardship could be very beneficial to you emotionally and spiritually.) So really, we need to check our hearts before spending.

3. *Giving*: 2 Corinthians 9:7 sums up how we stay pure in our giving. It says *"You should give what you have decided in your heart to give. You shouldn't give if you don't want to. You shouldn't give because you are forced to. God loves a cheerful giver."* (NIRV) God wants us to give out of the generosity of our hearts and he wants our giving to be a pleasant experience. If you find yourself giving out of obligation or coercion, don't do it until you have the right heart. Not to say you should never give if you're not 100% cheerful, but you know when your heart is not in it.

It's not our money; it's God's money. God created everything on this earth, including the trees to make the paper to make the money. So, in essence the money we make is not ours as He created us with the talents to be able to do that job that gives us a salary. We need to know that we are only stewards over the money that God has entrusted us with. Do you have the mentality that you are a steward or an owner of the money that comes into your hands? All our money comes from God and therefore belongs to him. A steward, which we are called to be, is someone who manages something. So, God invites us to manage the money He gives us in the way we spend it, give it away, and save it

Trust God in your finances. *Proverbs 3:5-6 states: "Trust in the Lord with all your heart. Do not depend on your own understanding. In all your ways obey him. Then he will make your paths smooth and straight."* (NIRV) Solomon couldn't have said it better, God wants us to trust him and not try to figure things out in our minds. When we trust God, we realize that He is the true Jehovah Jireh, our provider. God promises in His Word that He will supply for all our needs according to His riches in heaven.

(Philippians 4:19) This includes our finances. We need to stay pure in our finances by trusting God and knowing the He is our ultimate provider.

I encourage you to spend some time with God and ask him to search your heart to see if there are impurities when it comes to your finances. Perhaps these are new concepts for you, or ones that you are already doing. Wherever you are, my prayer is that you will learn how to seek, obtain and maintain purity in this area of your life.

CHAPTER 2: PURITY IN EMOTIONS

Anger

In order to understand our emotions, we have to first understand where our emotions come from. It is said that we are made up of three parts: mind, body and soul. In the spiritual sense we could say that we are spiritual beings living in a natural body that has a soul. Our soul is where our emotions come from.

Emotions are considered to be carnal in nature as opposed to the spiritual nature that lives inside us. The Bible teaches us to not allow these emotions to control our actions. Emotions tend to be reactive; they react to external stimuli (or in my case emotions can come out of nowhere other than to trip me up). Emotions can also be a great indicator of our heart's condition. Have you ever felt angry all of sudden, or get sad out of the blue? Emotions are great at navigating what our hearts are trying to tell us. That anger you feel could be an indicator that you are carrying around hurt in your heart, or that sadness could be unresolved grief that needs to be dealt with. These are mere examples, and may not be the case with your emotions. In any case, emotions are our body's way of telling us when something else is going on under the surface.

I was living with my parents at the time, planning to move out on my own very soon. I was in between jobs so my plans to move out were temporarily on hold. My parents had just told me that they had decided to downsize and wanted to sell the house, so they would be starting renovations soon in order to list it.

I remember it like it was yesterday, it was a Sunday in March, and I was asking my parents about their plans to start work on my bedroom as they were going to do renovations in there. What this required was me temporarily moving out of my room, and moving all my stuff into the bedroom in the basement. They were getting my younger brother to do the renovations, so that they can save some money. They didn't have a plan or answer for me and kept giving me the run around. So naturally I got upset, and I lost it; I lashed out in anger and said things I shouldn't have said. This resulted in me moving out of my parents' place a week later.

This is an extreme example, but oftentimes I would allow my emotions to get the better of me and in turn I would be left to pick up the pieces of a shattered relationship with my family members. In that particular moment I allowed my emotions to control my response. Like I said earlier, emotions are reactive- they normally react to outward stimuli- another person, a situation, etc. But God says in His Word that he has given us a way out; a choice. In Galatians 5, it lists all the fruits of the Holy Spirit that we benefit from, and one of them is self-control. (Galatians 5:23) That includes control over our emotions. As Paul is encouraging young Timothy he reminds him *"for God gave us a spirit not of fear but of power and love and self-control."* (2Timothy 1:7) So God has given us the means to control our reactive emotions. Therefore, we don't have to allow them to get the best of us.

There is no situation or temptation too great as Paul states to the church in Corinth: *"No temptation has overtaken you that is not common to man. God is faithful, and He will not let you be tempted beyond your ability, but with the temptation He will also provide the way of escape, that you may be able to endure it."* (1 Corinthians 10:13, ESV) God created us, knit us together in our mother's womb so He knows us and understands how we work; especially how our emotions work. (Psalm 139:14) He also knows that we are spiritual beings and by our spirits combined with the Holy Spirit we can overcome any carnal function in our bodies. Just because we experience an emotional response does not mean that we have to act upon those emotions.

Just because we experience an emotional response does not mean that we have to act upon those emotions.

Let's go back to my conversation with my parents. I got angry because they didn't have a definitive answer for me and I felt like there was no plan in place and I was going to be asked to uproot my life at any given moment with no warning. The background to that conversation was that I was in a very busy season of my life, and I was not at home very often. I am a planner and just wanted to plan out when I could make time to pack up my stuff and move it out of my room. With that said, there was a couple different ways that I could have handled that situation: I could have chosen to talk it out with them instead of lashing out according to my emotions or I could have removed myself from the situation as soon as I felt those emotions coming so as to calm down before I reengaged them. You see God calls us not to react, but to act. Make the right choice to not give into how we are feeling, and lay aside emotions in order to act according to His Word. 1 Peter 3:11 states *"Search for peace, and work to maintain it."* (NLT) I am confident that in the case with my parents if I were to act according to the Word of God, which is the sword of the spirit and not give in to my emotions, the way the conversation ended would have been very different. I want to challenge you to be someone that acts upon the Word of God as opposed to reacting to the world around you!

Anger has always been a big part of my life (it touched on every area), that in some ways it became a habit to me or for lack of a better term; a lifestyle. This had always been an area of struggle for me. As soon as I would deal with the cause of my anger it would appear in a different area of my life. This cycle carried on for years, until recently.

I was watching a video online and this speaker was talking about "cracks" in our lives. He defined these cracks as those areas of our lives that need God's presence and healing. Cracks are usually small, but when left unattended, can end up becoming big strongholds or setbacks in our lives. Then the speaker encouraged us to ask God if there were any cracks in our life and if He could come in and heal those areas to make us whole. Immediately I knew that it was one of those God moments- where God speaks directly to you through something/someone else. So, I proceeded to pray to God and asked him if there were any cracks in my life. Instantly, God revealed to me that I have one big crack and a few small cracks. The big crack was anger.

My anger started to come out at weird times. I would be driving and if someone in front of me made a wrong judgment or bad maneuver and I would find myself yelling at them wondering what in the heck they were thinking. My favourite line, and this I believe was my dad's influence, was "Did they get their license out of a cracker jack box?"

I had struggled with- dare I say it- road rage. You did not want to see me in the car. I would yell at other drivers, call them names and make all sorts of comments. Mind you all of that was done with the windows up so the other drivers wouldn't hear me. So, I wasn't actually confrontational as I was more of a closet road rager, but it was still a form of my anger coming out. It was not my proudest moment.

I sought God, got into my prayer closet and allowed God through His Holy Spirit to start to work in my heart in this area. God took me through a series of steps to overcome anger, and one of them was praying for freedom from acting out when I feel this emotion. (For more on gaining freedom from your emotions, check out Joyce Meyer's *Living Beyond Your Emotions*) Then he asked me to personalize Scriptures and declare them over myself every day. An example of this is:

I AM NOT AN ANGRY PERSON!

I will not sin by letting anger control me. I will think about it overnight and remain silent! - Psalm 4:4

God was showing me how to use the sword of the Spirit to combat and breakdown old cycles of emotional reactions, especially where anger was concerned.

WHAT I LEARNED

I know I have said that we are to choose not to act on our anger and take the higher road, but what does that look like practically? Well I asked God the same question. I knew in my own strength I would act upon my anger by taking full blown temper tantrums. It wasn't pretty for me and maybe this is you too. Anger became a habit for me. If we want to break a habit, what do we need to do? Replace it with another habit. Here are a couple tips that have worked for me:

Self-control is a fruit of the Holy Spirit. (Galatians 5:22-23) So therefore, in order for us to control our reaction to our emotions, we need to get into God's presence daily and get filled anew each day with the Holy Spirit. Part of the Lord's Prayer that Jesus taught us is to ask God to *"give us this day our daily bread."* (Matthew 6:11) I believe our daily bread is that part of the Holy Spirit we need for that day, the new fruit that will get us through the day.

We have a choice. Another part to not reacting to our emotions is simply choice. We have to choose how we will act when our emotions come. When I was younger, I used to say things like "I can't help it," "I feel it so strong, and then I react," or "It's burning inside of me and it has to come out some way or I'll burst!" All of those statements are true to me but, like I said, God's Word promises us self-control and also promises that there is no temptation that He hasn't already found a way out for us. So now, through Him, I can confidently say that reacting to our emotions is a choice and no excuse can be presented to debate otherwise. Deuteronomy 30:19 says *"I'm offering you the choice of life or death. You can choose either blessings or curses. But I want you to choose life."* (NLT) Moses had just finished going through all the blessings and curses that the Israelites would receive depending on whether they obeyed or disobeyed God's commands and at the end of it all he was urging all of them to choose life which is obedience to God and His laws. God wants the same for us. He wants us to choose life- choose to not give in to our emotions, choose to say no to anger and choose peace instead. (Just a side note: emotions are not meant to be a negative thing- they are the road map to the condition of our heart. So, if we are feeling negative or positive emotions, they are usually a symptom of a deeper heart issue.)

Removal. I found that when those negative emotions would start bubbling up that I would remove myself from the situation, conversation and just walk away.

Take a breath. Sometimes in the past I would find myself just taking a deep breath and counting to 10 if I felt a conversation getting heated. It helped me get refocused and not lose my cool.

The armour of God. Let's dig deeper, and look at the spiritual aspect of my strategy to controlling my anger: most of it came out when I was driving. I got worked up because someone cut me off or someone made selfish manoeuvre. Then I would yell at them in my car getting worked up. As I was praying about this I felt like God speak to me and tell me to put on the armour of God (Ephesians 6:13-19) every time I stepped into my car. More specifically, to put on the shoes of the gospel of peace. I had to work at spreading peace even to other drivers on the road. If I would suit up with the Holy Spirit every time I got into my car then I found I would keep my peace while driving. It has been working for me, but there are still times when I slip up. In those moments, I repent immediately and receive His grace.

Repent. Repentance is "a change of heart and mind that bring us closer to God. It includes turning away from sin and turning to God for forgiveness. It is motivated by love for God and a sincere desire to obey his commandments."[vii] When I lashed out in anger, I learned that repentance was the answer. Part of repentance is confession. In order for us to turn away from our sin, we need to remove it from our lives. We do this by confessing our sins to God. When we do, His Word says that He will forgive us all our sins. (1 John 1:9) Then, and only then we can open ourselves up to receive His grace and mercy to not sin again. A result of true repentance, our desire to turn away from sin, is our need to find practical ways (placing a Scripture card with the armour of God Scripture on it, personalizing Scripture and speaking them over our lives, etc.) to turn away from that, and this is the key to practically staying pure when anger arises.

Forgive. I realized that the reason I got angry with my friends and family was because I was carrying around hurts from a long time ago that I never forgave those people for. Colossians 3:13 states plainly: *"Forgive one another if you are holding something against someone. Forgive, just as the Lord forgave you."* The Greek word for forgive in this verse is *charizomai*, which literally translates to: grace, extending favour, freely give favour.[viii] Well that's exactly what God did for us. When we were knee deep in our darkness and sin, He extended His favour on us so that we might experience right relationship with him (Romans 5:8). God wants us to forgive others not for their sake, but for His and ours. He extended favour to us first, so we should extend that same favour to others. He wants us to do this, so that we can be free from the emotional baggage we end up carrying around from those hurts (more about that later in the chapter).

Every day I speak the words "I am not an angry person" over my life and allow the Holy Spirit to do its work in me. You see, when I finally allowed God to deal with those deeper issues that were causing the anger, I was freed to start practically dealing with the symptoms of the anger. Until I actually dealt with the root I couldn't deal with the symptoms. I am so thankful that God has freed me from my anger and I can say for the first time in my life, that I am *truly* not an angry person anymore! (Side note: I still feel angry from time to time, but I am free from spiritual bondage that lead me to react in sin when I felt angry. Now I get to choose how I will react and make the right decisions.) I am free and am walking out my purity in anger.

Offense

Let's take emotions one step further and delve into the world of offense. It's important to note that being offended or carrying an offense is not an actual feeling or emotion, but a choice of action as a result of a feeling. It's a transitive verb (meaning it's something that is done to us). The Mariam Webster dictionary defines the word offend "to cause (a person or group) to feel hurt, angry, or upset by something said or done."[ix] The verb *offend* is done to us and the noun *offense*, is the choice proceeding the verb. In essence we choose to hold offense because we have been offended (aka felt hurt, upset or angry).

The story I am about to tell you is based on real events and I have just changed the names of the people involved and a little bit of the situation. I remember this like it was yesterday. I had an argument with a friend and words were exchanged. Basically, the gist of it was that she had expectations of me and I didn't live up to them. I am the type of person that if you want me to do something, just ask. I am pretty reasonable and I will usually do what you want me to do. However, this was not the case here. We had one of the arguments that left us both feeling like we got smacked in the face.

A couple of days later, she asked to meet up so that we could try and resolve this. I was hopeful for resolution, so with a pep in my step and a bit of trepidation, we met. Let me preface this by saying that this was not one of those conversations where we met, and she said sorry, and I said sorry and we all lived happily ever after. Oh no, this was very different. As we sat, she proceeded to take out a paper with some notes on it. She then started to read off a list of my faults and shortcomings, using the paper as reference. She said that these may be blind spots and these are areas of my life that I needed to work on. If anyone knows me, they know I have a hard time coming to term with my own shortcomings when pointed out by the Holy Spirit. I really didn't receive anything she had to say as I was in so much shock and I was mega offended. All I could was cry. Unfortunately, that was the end of our friendship. (Side note: If you ever want to point out a friend's shortcomings, please do it in love. Talk it through with a mentor- which I believe she did, and pray, pray, pray about it. If God is telling you to hold off, it's for a reason. You want that other person to feel loved as they are being corrected.)

Years later, I found myself bringing up this offense in a conversation, realizing that I was still not over it. Now I am finally over it and I am able to see this person and truly wish them well. But it wasn't easy.

You see, the thing with offense is that when it's left and not dealt with, something happens: we end up becoming bitter. One small offense that can easily be dealt with (in my case it was a bigger offense) turns into anger, which when left untreated, becomes bitterness and takes root in our hearts.

The Hebrew word for 'offense' is *proskomma*, which literally translated means "stumbling block or that over which a soul stumbles i.e. by which is caused to sin."[x] So this proskomma is something that prevents us from living the life that Jesus died and rose again to give us- that abundant life. (John 10:10) That offense that we are holding onto is affecting every area of our lives. If we are not careful, it could end up causing us to ultimately stumble spiritually. If we do fall, which we will, because let's face it, we are not perfect, God promises that we won't fall. He has us. (Psalm 37:24) So take heart that even though we have tripped up by this thing called "offense", that we won't ultimately fall spiritually.

WHAT I LEARNED

So, you're probably wondering how we live a life of purity when we get offended? Continual forgiveness, as Jesus has called us to do. If we go back to Lord's prayer that Jesus taught his disciples, he said in verses 12 and 14, *"And forgive us our debts, as we forgive our debtors...For if you forgive men their trespasses, your heavenly Father will also forgive you."* (Matthew 6:12 &14, NKJV) This call for action instructs us to first and foremost forgive those who have made us hurt, angry or upset. Once we do that, then we are free to receive God's forgiveness for us. How can we expect to be forgiven if we can't forgive others?

Choose mercy every day. Furthermore, Paul urges the Colossian church in Colossians 3:12 to *"put on tender mercies"* (NKJV), or as another version puts it *"compassionate hearts,"* (ESV) as we have been chosen by God. Moreover, the Amplified Bible Classic Bible version says it like this:

"Clothe yourselves therefore, as God's own chosen ones (His own picked representatives), [who are] purified and holy and well-beloved [by God Himself, by putting on behavior marked by] tenderhearted pity and mercy, kind feeling, a lowly opinion of yourselves, gentle ways, [and] patience [which is tireless and long-suffering, and has the power to endure whatever comes, with good temper]."

As God's chosen people, purified and holy, God wants us to put on mercy so when someone hurts us or upsets us, we can choose to forgive them.

Just forgive! I talked about it before. It has always been a sticky subject, especially in cases where it does not warrant forgiveness (murder, crime, abuse, etc.). These crimes are done out of spite and on purpose. Yes, it pains me to say it, but even those people should be forgiven. God wants us to forgive everyone, period end of story, no matter how brutal the sin. I'm not saying their sin is admissible or even likeable, but Jesus died on the cross for all of us, even the most heinous sinners. That means that they too should be forgiven, which I understand requires a lot of grace (God's unmerited favour) to be poured out on us doing the forgiving and those being forgiven. God poured out His grace on us when we least deserved it- when we were knee deep in our own sin. There were probably things that we did that deeply offended God. Remember when He chose to love us by pulling us out of our dark pits.

Someone once said unforgiveness is like "drinking poison and expecting the other person to suffer." Well the reality of that situation is that the only person that ends up getting hurt is us. When we choose not to forgive, it only poisons us and usually doesn't affect the other person. We usually believe the other person deserves to suffer for our suffering but by holding onto that anger or hurt against someone else, we inevitably only end up hurting ourselves. Remember, it doesn't affect the other person if you don't forgive them, it only affects you.

As stated before we must forgive those we have a complaint against. (Colossians 3:13) Basically, since God has forgiven us, we must forgive others. It's that simple! When we feel upset, angry or hurt we can choose to react with forgiveness. Let me clarify in saying that forgiveness does not mean forgetting; it means letting go. It doesn't mean replaying the hurt(s) in your head and getting yourself upset again and again. You can choose to forgive that person, let go and move on.

Have compassion. Jesus was constantly moved by compassion when he would see the hurt, the sick, and the sinners. He forgave the woman who committed adultery because of His compassion for her (John 8:11). Sometimes when someone hurts us it's not always out of spite, it could be for other reasons we can't really see in the moment. It helps to learn a little bit more about: what actually upsets/angers/hurts us, what has the other person been through, who are they (they may have hurt you because they themselves were hurting), and what is the situation (Is there anything I can do to avoid offense in that moment?). With a little bit of wisdom and insight, we can choose to let that offense go and move on and maybe even extend grace to the other party involved. After all, we are all in need of grace from time to time.

Doubt

In order to truly understand a concept or anything for that matter (in this case doubt), we need to look at the definition of it. Doubt means: "to be uncertain," or "to lack confidence in."[xi] Uncertainty or lack of confidence are emotions, doubt is a state of being that leads to impure emotions. Therefore, doubt itself is actually not an emotion, but it causes us to feel impure emotions. This goes directly against how God has called us to live in confidence and certainty. If purifying our lives means to remove all impurities, I would argue that doubt is an impurity that we need to get rid from our hearts. More specifically, doubt in God, His ability and in what He is doing in our lives. God calls us to focus on whatever is pure. (Philippians 4:8) Emotional purity can only come from God and His Word, therefore any emotional response that doesn't line up with His Word, is impure.

The Bible describes a person who doubts as someone who "is like a wave of the sea that is driven and tossed by the wind. For that person must not suppose that he will receive anything from the Lord; he is a double-minded man, unstable in all his ways." (James 1:6-8) James describes doubt as a double-mindedness; having two conflicting schools of thought at the same time. According to James, doubt makes you unclear, so when you ask God for something with doubt in your heart, you will not receive it. When we doubt, we rob ourselves of the faith that God so richly has blessed us with to believe that we will receive that thing we asked for. Simply put, when we doubt, we are basically saying to God that we don't believe that He is going to come through the same time we are asking him for that thing. We are canceling out our request and therefore cannot be expected to receive anything. Doubt is the absence of faith in the midst of desire. So, we can conclude that faith is the opposite of doubt.

Since I was a little girl I was always a big dreamer- head in the clouds, imagining a better life for myself. Dreaming big usually requires big faith. Normally when I would set my mind to something, I just knew I would achieve it. There was no stopping me once I got an idea into my head. I remember I wanted to move to toe shoes in my ballet class, I was determined. I would do foot strengthening exercises and wear my toe shoes constantly at home. Finally, my ballet teacher gave into my consistent nagging and saw my hard work, then started training me on toe shoes.

When I wanted to pursue my postgraduate studies in England, I was determined then too- I placed sticky notes all around my room that had the words "I AM GOING TO ENGLAND!" in big bold letters on them. I only applied to just one university; that's how confident I was. I ended up getting into that University. Then there was funding, I didn't have enough money to go, but I had made a resolve that I was going to go and I was going to make it happen any way I knew how. I got the funding, moved out there and ended up living there for four and half years. Crazy audacious faith seemed innate to me as it paired well with my crazy big dreams. What's the use of having big dreams if you don't have the faith to believe that they will come true?

I share all of this to say that even though "faith," or more so believing in the impossible to happen, came naturally to me, it does not mean that I didn't struggle with doubt ever. Before I came to Jesus it was easy to have faith in myself, I didn't know any better; it was never really tested. But once I learned about another type of faith that comes from God, a faith that can move mountains (Matthew 17:20), I had to learn to protect and nurture that faith.

Since doubt is impurity, and the absence of doubt is faith, then faith is what we need to purify our minds. We know that faith comes from God, and that He gives us all our own measure. (Romans 12:3) So we need God in order purify our minds in this area of doubt. In order for us to produce faith and for it to grow and mature, we need troubles. Peter states in 1 Peter 1:7-8, that *"These trials will show that your faith is genuine. It is being tested as fire tests and purifies gold—though your faith is far more precious than mere gold. So, when your faith remains strong through many trials, it will bring you much praise and glory and honor on the day when Jesus Christ is revealed to the whole world."* (NLT) We must be aware that true faith is tested. (James 1:3-5)

Jesus makes it clear in Matthew 21:21: *"And Jesus answered them, "Truly, I say to you, if you have faith and do not doubt, you will not only do what has been done to the fig tree, but even if you say to this mountain, 'Be taken up and thrown into the sea,' it will happen."* (ESV) Jesus was referring to what just happened when He spoke to the fig tree and how it shriveled up on his command. (Matthew 21:19, ESV) So essentially in the absence of doubt, we can move mountains! What a cool concept! If we didn't have doubt, I wonder what else we could achieve in our lives?

In my early 20's I set out on a journey of self-discovery that lead me to the arms of an ever-loving God just five years later. Fast forward a couple years

I felt my once strong faith I had as little girl being reactivated and changed into something new. All of a sudden, I felt like there was hope in my life, that my life had a purpose, and that it was okay to dream because there was a chance that it could come true. In my new-found relationship, I started asking God for things and actually found myself believing in Him for them. He would deliver, and it almost seemed like it was instant at that time.

Here I am eight years into my journey and my faith is being tested. A few years ago, at the beginning of the year, I was praying and asking God for a word for the year. (Side note: If you have never done that or heard about it, I suggest you do it- it's changed my life. It's called Get One Word, and it runs on the premise that you pray and seek God for a word/theme that will set the tone and help you focus your year ahead). God gave me the word "run." As he spoke that to me, he whispered something else into my heart: "you are ready." I asked him to clarify what He meant by the words "you are ready," having a pretty good guess of what He was talking about. I believed God was saying that I was ready to put myself out there relationally. My first reaction was "No way, I am not ready!" Then I quickly began to doubt that God even spoke to me. I then questioned how I could be ready, because at the time my life was all over the place (my parents were on the brink of a divorce, I was about to move out of my current place and had no idea where I was going next, and my finances were not in order.) I was the definition of a mess. So, doubt was my first response when God called me to get out there relationally. Then I decided to run away from the whole thing and just avoid it all together. Fast-forward to the end of the year and I finally started to accept and believe in the word God gave me earlier.

So, if my word was "you are ready," I decided to do what any good Christian would, I prayed about how I how I would put myself out there. Well I believe God spoke to me about online dating. One of the main reasons I decided to go online was when I had the thought about doing it fear arose in me. I was not going to let fear stop me from stepping into my future or meeting my future husband, so I went online. Unfortunately, it only helped me discover what I wasn't looking for. The experience lasted a mere couple of months and I found myself cancelling my subscription a year later.

So, doubt started to creep in again about God's word. I prayed "God you gave me this word and I asked you what it meant and I believe it was about relationships. But nothing happened when I put myself out there. Is that what you actually meant?" To this day as I write this, I am still unsure why I experienced that. A few months later, I found a new hope in the area of relationships. Just because nothing happened the year before, it didn't mean God was not moving in this area of my life. My faith was reignited once again. At that time, I set out to learn as much as I could on the subject of marriage: what did the Bible say? What did the world say? What did others who were married have to say? What did experts on the subject of marriage have to say? I was curious and wanted to learn more. This exploration of information kept my faith alive, and kept my hopes up.

Jeremiah 29:11 states: *"I know the plans I have for you," announces the LORD. "I want you to enjoy success. I do not plan to harm you. I will give you hope for the years to come."* (NIRV) How many of us have heard this Scripture time and time again and have glossed over it with an attitude of "Oh yeah, I know that God has a plan for me, to give me hope." I admit that the older I get, the harder it gets to believe that God will bring a husband for me. As a woman in her mid-thirties who wants to get married and have children, I feel that my weakened faith is justified. However, if we read that Scripture again, I see that God wants to give me a hope, not temporary, but lasting, and He doesn't want to harm me- God only has good for me. So, if I find it hard to believe that God is going to send me a mate, then I can find solace in his Word that says this trial is testing and purifying my faith to make it even stronger. Simply my faith needs to increase. Like I said before, faith is the absence of doubt.

WHAT I LEARNED

So, you're probably thinking, "Amanda, how do we increase our faith?" Well I had that same question when I realized that my faith was weak.

The Word of God. Romans 10:17 tells us *"So then faith comes by hearing, and hearing by the word of God."* What helped me in this those early days when the desire was strongest, was reading the Bible and studying what it had to say about the subject of promises (looking to God's promise of marriage- more on that later). And then I started to pray that Word over my life daily. If faith comes from hearing the Word of God, then we need to speak it into our lives every day. If all I ever hear is "I am single, I will never get married, I'm too old to get married," how can my faith grow to a point where I am believing that "God has a mate handpicked for me, I will get married."

Align your faith with God's ability. As Moses writes in Numbers 23:19 *"God is not a man, so he does not lie. He is not human, so he does not change His mind. Has he ever spoken and failed to act? Has he ever promised and not carried it through?"* (NLT) You see I had a choice to make, I could either allow doubt to cloud my faith or I could bring my faith in line with God's ability. Since I already knew that God can do exceedingly and abundantly above anything I can ask or think, (Ephesians 3:20) I brought my faith in line with a God who can do the impossible. So once again I sought out the Word of God to see what it said about God's promises and who God was regarding the fulfillment of promises.

Prayer. For a season in order to fuel my faith and remember who God was and what He was capable of, I would pray this prayer over my life every day:

Daddy [this is my term for our heavenly Father- it always makes me feel like His daughter when I call him this], You are the Lord my God. I desire to love you, listen to Your voice, and hold fast to you, for you, Lord, are my life (Deuteronomy 30:20). Daddy, you are great and powerful. Glory, majesty and beauty belong to you. Everything in heaven and on earth is yours. Even the Kingdom belongs to you. You are honoured as the One who rules over all. (1 Chronicles 29:11) In your hand is the life of every creature and the breath of all mankind (Job 12:10). You, my God, open Your hand and satisfy the desires of every living thing (Psalm 145:16). Daddy, since the creation of the world Your invisible qualities- Your eternal power and divine nature- have been clearly seen, being understood from what has been made, so that men are without excuse (Romans 1:20). O, merciful Father, help me not to exchange the truth of God for a lie, and worship and serve created things rather than you, our Creator- who is forever praised (Romans 1:25). O, God, my God, help me never to worship any other God, for you Daddy, are a jealous God (Exodus 20:4-5). Daddy, Heaven is your throne and the Earth is your footstool (Isaiah 66:1). I acknowledge that your thoughts are not my thoughts, neither are your ways my ways. As the heavens are higher than the earth, so are your ways higher than my ways, and your thoughts higher than my thoughts (Isaiah 55:8-9). Daddy, you are not a man that you should lie, not a son of man, that you should change your mind. I thank you that when you speak, you act. And what you promise, you fulfill (Numbers 23:19). Daddy, you are my God, and I will exalt you and praise your name, for in perfect faithfulness you have done marvellous things, things planned long ago (Isaiah 25:1). Now to the King eternal, immortal, invisible, the only God, be honour and glory forever and ever, Amen (1 Timothy 1:17).[xii]

I would pray that over my life and into ever area where I doubted God to move in and in turn built up my faith to match our ever loving, always faithful God. (Side note: Notice how this prayer talks about who God is and His nature? It reminded me daily of the God I served, the God who was able to do the impossible, the God who was in control, the God who was going to do what He said he will do in my life.) It's important to pray, especially for those things that have not yet manifested in the natural. I believe prayer is giving God the go ahead to release in the spiritual what has yet to happen in the natural. In other words, by taking something to God, we are surrendering it to Him so that He can begin to move on our behalf to help it come to pass in our lives. So, praying God's promises into your life- in this case marriage- is releasing God to move on behalf of you in this area of your life.

By using the Word of God, aligning our faith with God's ability and praying, we can win the battle to purify our emotions in the area of doubt. Let our faith grow through the Word of God so that we stop doubt in its tracks from polluting our hearts. Let me encourage you to find a few Scriptures about God's promises for you that ignite your faith and be diligent in praying them over your life. You could even take it one step further and pray that future into existence, your future marriage into existence. Call it forth by strengthening your faith in God's Word.

Fear

The dictionary defines fear as "an unpleasant often strong emotion caused by anticipation or awareness of danger."[xiii] Off the bat we already know that fear is an emotion, but obviously not one that we won't to experience. We also get from this definition that fear is an indication of something going on in us. Usually fear is coupled with the fact that we feel threatened, in danger or like something painful is coming our way. I would argue for the purposes of this book that fear is an impure emotion as it goes against the Word of God.

Paul encourages Timothy in 2 Timothy 1:7: *"God has not given us a spirit of fear and timidity, but of power, love, and self-discipline."* In essence, because we have the Spirit of the living God on the inside of us, we should not fear. Fear merely pollutes our hearts by taking our focus away from God.

When I got into my teenage years, a whole new fear arose in me. Thoughts of: "Was I good enough? Do people like me? Am I worthy of friendship? What if everyone hates me? What if people are mean to me? What if I fail in school?" riddled my mind as I went through high school. High school for me wasn't the great experience you hear about. For me it was a battlefield. I was happy if I could make it through a day of school not being noticed; that way no one would be able to put me down, make fun of me or bully me- at least that's what I thought. Well unfortunately, I did not escape bullying. This girl and her friends who were all two years younger than me found it their job to bully me every day on my way home from school. It's like bullies smell fear and go for the person that they know has the most fear. It's twenty years later and I know for certain how true that statement is. Bullies tend to use your fear against you so that they can keep you where you need to be- below them or under their influence. So, on top of dealing with being a teenager, added to that was a legit fear for my safety. I didn't feel safe walking home or roaming the halls of school. Fearful thoughts filled my head and it stopped me from doing a lot of things in my life. I almost felt like I was trapped in a prison of fear in my mind. Bottom line, fear ruled my life.

WHAT I LEARNED

Then I broke free! You see I got to know a man that supersedes any emotion or feeling I could feel, a man that showed me that His love for me overshadowed any wrong thing I could do, a man that extended grace when I was living in darkness and decided to pull me into the light. That man's name is Jesus. The main thing Jesus taught was love. Romans 8:39 states: *"... absolutely nothing can get between us and God's love because of the way that Jesus our Master has embraced us."* (MSG) So, no matter what happened to me in high school or when I was younger, none of that mattered- Jesus still loved me. That revelation rocked my world and was the first step in me breaking free from fear in my life.

Fear works the same way a bully works. It preys on the weak (those struggling with fear) and thrives off of fear (by giving us more fear). When we allow fear to control our lives, we attract more fear. Plus, since fear is an emotion, it's all in our heads. So, although fear is real to us, others who can't see it can't understand those fears. So, by nature fear isolates us. And that's exactly what the enemy wants; for us to be isolated in our own thought life. I encourage you that if you are struggling with fear, tell someone. Bring out into the light that thing that is hidden in the dark. (Ephesians 5:11) Don't give it any more power than it already has over you.

1 John 4:18 says, *"There is no room in love for fear. Well-formed love banishes fear. Since fear is crippling, a fearful life is one not yet fully formed in love."* (MSG) This verse tells us three things about love and fear:

There is no room in love for fear. This is pretty self-explanatory. Fear has no place in us when we are filled with God's love- His perfect love pushes out all fear from inside of us.

Well-formed love banishes fear. The word banish means: to drive out or force out.[xiv] So when we are filled with the love of God, it forces out all fear from the inside of us. The two cannot co-exist.

A fearful life is one not yet fully formed in love. Another version puts it as *"not fully experienced his perfect love."* (NLT) So we need to get a revelation of God's perfect love or fully formed love living on the inside of us first, in order to give fear its eviction papers and send that emotion packing. That can only come from getting to know our Creator- through His Word, worship and prayer.

Ultimately, we all need to remember, *"God has not given us a spirit of fear and timidity, but of power, love, and self-discipline."* (2 Timothy 1:7, NLT) The Spirit that God placed inside of us when we came to faith is of power, love and self-discipline and since we already know that God's perfect, well-formed love banishes fear, we can live in true freedom from fear and live a life of purity.

CHAPTER 3: PURITY IN RELATIONSHIPS

Relationships are a two-way street; they are give and take and ebb and flow. I have learned that some relationships are meant to last and while others are just for a season. Relationships help us grow as we learn to live together. If done correctly, relationships help us not to be so selfish. Purity in relationships can be a tricky achievement. It would look different with each relationship you are in, whether that is husband/wife, brother/sister, mother/father, aunt/uncle, etc. So, what does it actually look like? The following are the types of relationships that when lived out in purity can lead to a very fulfilling life.

Self

When I was a young girl I struggled with self-esteem. I always doubted who I was and if anyone challenged my character I would crumble under the pressure of their test. I was empty on the inside and didn't know myself at all. Plus, I really didn't want to get to know myself because based on the opinions of those around me I wasn't worth getting to know. I mean, I didn't even like hanging out with me so why would others? Sounds sad doesn't it? Well that's who I was on the inside, until I realized I didn't want to live like that anymore. I started on a journey to truly get to know who I was, to find myself, discover who I truly was meant to be. I always thought the person I was, was not the person that I know I could be or who I was meant to be. I saw others and how confident they were and how they were living these great lives and here I was stuck inside my head; doubting everything and every*one* around me, afraid to make even one move for fear of failure.

On that night of the beginning of my journey to true discovery of who I really was, I grabbed a pen and a pad of paper and decided to document everything that uniquely made up who I was. I wrote down all my likes, dislikes of food, colours, activities, strengths and weaknesses, past relationships, etc. (Side note: if you have never done anything like this before. I dare you to try it! This exercise is great for getting to know who you are. Especially if like me you struggle with self-esteem and self-worth issues. It helps you understand who you are more, your likes, dislikes, what you want in life and what you are willing to put with. It creates a foundation for a great relationship with you!)

Five years after I wrote that list, I came to faith and it was my faith in God that helped me realize who I truly was: I am loved, I am worthy of love and nothing can separate me from that love. The first Word that I ever received from God was Romans 8:38-39:

None of this fazes us because Jesus loves us. I'm absolutely convinced that nothing—nothing living or dead, angelic or demonic, today or tomorrow, high or low, thinkable or unthinkable—absolutely nothing can get between us and God's love because of the way that Jesus our Master has embraced us. (MSG)

That revelation got me right in the heart and I was changed forever. For the first time in my life, somebody wanted me. Someone was paying attention to me for the right reason. And no matter what I did, thought or said, nothing could separate me from that love. Wow! What an amazing discovery.

I want to say that after that amazing discovery all my self esteem and self worth issues just disappeared, but that took time and work on my part. The years that followed had me still struggling with my self-worth. Herein started my journey to truly discovering who I was through the eyes of God. I remember someone saying to me that I needed to know who God says I am to truly know who I am. So that's what I did, I found all the things that God said about who I was in the Bible:

I am a new creation in Christ! (2 Corinthians 5:17)

I am chosen. I am holy. (1 Peter 2:9)
I am God's very own possession. (Galatians 2:20)
I am God's beloved. (John 15:15)
I am a friend of God. (John 1:12)
I am a child of God. (Galatians 3:26)
I am an heir to God's glory. (Romans 8:17)
I am a citizen of heaven. (Philippians 3:20)
God gave His one and only son for me. God loves me so much. (John 3:16)
I am the temple of God. (1 Corinthians 3:16)
I am more than a conqueror. (Romans 8:37)
I am fearfully and wonderfully made. God knew me before I was born. He knit me
together in the womb. (Psalm 139:13-16)
God has a plan for my life. (Jeremiah 29:11)
I am created in God's image. (Genesis 1:27)
I am chosen by God. I was adopted into God's family. (Ephesians 1:4-5)
I am saved by God. God has identified me as His own. God wants to give me His inheritance. (Ephesians 1:13-14)
The hairs on my head are counted. I am valuable to God. (Luke 12:7)
I am God's masterpiece! (Ephesians 2:10)
I am a member of God's family! (Ephesians 2:19)
(*See image in Appendix B*)

Each day I would read these statements out loud. I did that for about a month and with the busyness of life, stopped and forgot about it. From time to time I would pull out that list when I was feeling my self-worth threatened, but hadn't really gotten these truths into my heart.

When I was in the No More GAGA program, the second type of relationship we focused on was relationship with self. If you aren't comfortable with yourself or love who you are, how can you expect others to want to be with you or love you? I had to get to know who I was after I had solidified my relationship with God. I knew who God said I was, but who was I really?

Slowly but surely, I started to view myself through the eyes of my Creator, made perfectly flawed. As I worked through my insecurities one by one, I began to accept me for who I was. I started to see how unique God actually made me and started, for the first time ever in my life, truly loving who I was. I was always afraid to be alone, because I didn't enjoy my own company. That changed and I found myself going to the movies by myself and just being intentional in spending time alone. I live on my own now, so I spend a lot of time by myself and I can now say that I truly enjoy my own company.

WHAT I LEARNED

Define your boundaries. Through a series of exercises, I had done I discovered who I was. Like before, I did up lists of my favourite things, habits, talents, skills, etc. The most important list I created was the one with my boundaries- defining how far I would go and was willing to let others around me go. (Side note: for a great resource on boundaries, check out the book: Boundaries by Dr. John Townsend and Dr. Henry Cloud. They take you through a similar exercise.) The book defines a boundary as something that "define(s) *what is me* and *what is not me*. A boundary shows me where I end and someone else begins, leading me to a sense of ownership." (pp.31) I created a list of boundaries for every area of my life (personal, relationships, dating, physical, financial, parenting, etc. These lists defined what I was and was not willing to put up with or tolerate.

An example of one of my personal boundaries was that I don't want to live with pets- never have and never had the desire to. I have severe allergies to cat and dog hair, and so did my mom so it's not something that I ever wanted to do. Plus, I just don't want to live with pets. Another example is: I am a traveler. Simply put, one day I would like to travel the world full time. I have always loved travelling, and travel will always be part of my lifestyle-that's who I am and what makes me uniquely me! This was one of my first steps in getting to know who I truly was.

Healing past hurts. One of those steps God led me to take brought me to the root of my insecurity, which affected every area of my life, including my self-worth. For fear of not liking the person who stared back at me in the mirror, I avoided getting to truly know and accept who I was.

I remember feeling, not really sure what was going on inside of me. This happened for a couple weeks. I knew I was struggling with something spiritually and as I prayed and asked God to show me what it was, it would come out in outbursts of anger, bad attitudes to co-workers and negative thoughts. Have you ever had that before; you know you are off, but you're not sure why? You ask God, but He doesn't really reveal anything to you all the while the feelings attached to this thing inside of you are being intensified.

One night God got a hold of me, when I was finally still enough to listen to what He was saying, and He showed me what was happening. He gave me a vision of a tree, and that tree had roots, and all the roots came from one seed. That seed was bad- it was what I was wrestling with. God was bringing it to the surface so that He could remove it from me. God revealed to me that I had a root of fear in my life that intersected and infiltrated every area of my life: relational, personal, physical, spiritual, financial, etc. It also caused every bad emotion/feeling I had or was experiencing in those two weeks.

After discussion with my pastor, we decided that she would take me through a set of prayers and questions to facilitate the uncovering of any root that may be holding me back from having an unblemished relationship with God. Near the end of the session, God revealed a spirit of self-rejection. This made total sense to me, because I had rejected me and who I was my whole life. It made so much sense to me, I was always afraid of being rejected so I would reject myself before anyone else could.

I want to encourage you that if you think you are dealing with past hurts or pains, ask God for help in starting the healing process. He wants us to be whole and free from all impurities.

Seek God. In the weeks that followed I sought God for a revelation of His perfect love. Since the seed of fear was broken in my life, and God's perfect love casts out all fear (1John 4:18), I knew I had to get a deeper revelation of that perfect love. God began to show me the different facets of His perfect love. Here are some truths that he showed me:

God's love is perfect- it's everything it needs to be to us when we need it; it's grace, mercy, peace, wisdom, knowledge, clarity, healing, comfort, and safety. Beauty for ashes (Isaiah 61:3a): The darkness on the inside of us has been replaced by His light. The dirt has been replaced by beauty, because of His perfect love living on the inside of us.

His perfect love is the same as I AM- just as powerful! It is the love of all loves- the greatest love.

All our anger, judgment, jealousy, ungratefulness, bitterness, etc.- every negative emotion belongs to God. Jesus gladly took it all upon himself at the cross- that's His perfect love for us.

There is no sin too overwhelming for God's love. His perfect love overshadows every sin.

Through those weeks I realized that truly nothing can separate me from God's perfect love. I am learning to love me. I heard once that "You attract the love that you think that you deserve."[xv] So how can I attract love I never had for myself? The only way to love myself is to fully accept the perfect love that God has for me. Through God we will begin to see our flaws through a lens of grace and our blemishes through a lens of love. Try it yourself, ask God to show you who you are, not the way you see yourself, but how He sees you. I'm positive that your world will be changed forever the way mine was.

Family

Just over four years ago marked the beginning of a series of events that changed my life forever. Remember the story I told you about how I got in an argument with my parents regarding renovations? Well there was a lot more to that story. My story picks up after that argument with my parents. A couple months went by without neither of us talking to each other. Then out of the blue I received a call from my father letting me know that he had left my mother. This started an 18-month battle, which ended in my parents getting a divorce. After almost 37 years they both decided to call it quits. That hit me pretty hard. As usual, everyone grieves in their own ways and this was no different. This sent a rift in my whole family.

I found myself trying to be the saviour of my family and took it upon myself to keep everyone together when I was barely holding on by a thread. I mean I was always the kid whose parents were not divorced and now that had all changed. I was angry with both my parents for just giving up after being married for so long. I was devastated that our family was being ripped apart.

Fast forward almost four years after my parents' divorce and things are just not the same. Certain family members still don't even talk and we are all dealing with our grief, hurts and pain. There is one thing I know in all of this: God is in control. I can be certain that He sees all of this and is working it all out for our good. Our story is not done. Sure, it doesn't look the way I want it to, but I live by my faith and not my sight. In the meantime, I will continue to pray and seek God in this situation with my family.

WHAT I LEARNED

I have learned a lot in the last four years about fighting, striving and maintaining purity in my familial relationships. Here a few things that helped me in my family's difficult season:

Persistent prayer. I have to say that one of the things that got me through this rough season was prayer; persistent prayer to be exact. Jesus tells the parable, in the book of Luke, about the persistent widow. It's about a woman who persistently asked the judge for justice. He didn't care about people so it seemed that he didn't really work hard to bring about justice for the people in a timely fashion. But because he was so annoyed with her constant asking, he finally caved and gave her the justice that she persistently desired.

Then the Lord said, *"Learn a lesson from this unjust judge. Even he rendered a just decision in the end. So, don't you think God will surely give justice to His chosen people who cry out to him day and night? Will he keep putting them off? I tell you, he will grant justice to them quickly!"* (Luke 18:6-8, NLT)

Jesus is encouraging us to be persistent in prayer and don't back down. In verse 1, Luke says *"always pray and never give up."* (Luke 18:1, NLT) God promises in His Word that he would bring about justice quickly compared to an earthly judge who doesn't care about people.

I prayed for my family every day, that we would overcome our anger towards each other, that there would be peace in my family and that God would most importantly restore our relationships. After my parents' divorce my brother and I stopped talking for a season. I felt the Lord challenge me to pray for and speak life over him for 40 days and 40 nights. That's exactly what I did. Every day I would ask the Holy Spirit to reveal to me what He wanted me to pray into my brother's life. When I finished praying for that time period, God moved in a mighty way. My mother was planning a family get together on Valentine's Day at my grandmother's place as it fell during

Family Day weekend. It turned out from all the children of the family my brother and I were the only ones who could make it. Well my brother talked to me that day; it was like nothing ever happened. God answered my persistent prayers to restore our relationship and now we are at peace. Something very similar happened with my younger brother, and although we are not as close as I would like us to be, I continue praying for him every day, having confidence that God will restore our relationship as well.

Paul asked the Colossians to *"be persistent and devoted to prayer, being alert and focused in your prayer life with an attitude of thanksgiving"* (Colossians 4:2, AMP). So, I challenge you that if your family is going through a rough season to get on your knees and start praying to God, the only one who can turn your situation around. God promises in His Word that He will answer our persistent prayers and much sooner than that judge did for that widow.

Love (practically). My one-word theme word a few years ago was 'love.' But not just any love, a love that is tangible and can be seen by others. The Scripture that God gave me to focus on that year was 1John 3:18: *"Little children, let's not love with words or speech but with action and truth."* (CEB) God was challenging me to actually show love to others and not just say I love them.

During a week of prayer and fasting that I participated in with my church, God gave me a revelation about His love and loving others: it's only when we get filled with God's love can we truly love on others. (See Fasting resource) I know it sounds simple, but in that moment, it was a rhema word (a rhema word is literally a Christ utterance. A word received from God by the Holy Spirit), it hit me right between the eyes. In 1 John 4:19 it states that *"We love because God first loved us."* In order for us to love others we need to have God's love in us. So, during that week it became my prayer that God would give me a deeper revelation of His love.

Well, be careful what you ask for. At 3:41 am on Wednesday of that week, in the stillness of the morning, God gently woke me up to speak words of love into my heart. God showed me that I belonged; that there was a place in His heart that only I could fit in. He longed to spend time with me, He pursued me, chased after me, and that I was His. This deeply impacted me as many times in my life I felt like I never belonged. I always felt like I was different, but God made sure in that moment that I knew deep down in my heart that I belonged to him and I always would.

During the week of prayer and fasting I also began to pray and ask God to give me practical ways that I could love those around me. An example of this was to become closer with my family. My grandmother had just turned 89 and she wasn't getting any younger, so I wanted to be intentional with making time to spend with her on a weekly basis. Now this is pretty huge for me as I was never really close with my grandmother growing up, but I wanted to change that.

So, at my grandmother's birthday party I announced to my family that I will be coming to her place to have lunch with my grandmother once a week and invited them to join us if they wanted to. I remember the first time I spent with her and I as spoke to her on the phone and told her I was coming over I could hear the excitement in her voice. I knew that that one small gesture of love: spending time with her, whether that meant sitting down and eating lunch together or watching Matlock with her, meant so much.

God also showed me that we can love others, not by big sweeping gestures, but by those small actions and moments. That is true purity in relationships, the small acts of love, it's in the routine of always being there for someone. And it's through those small actions and moments that she knows that I love her. After continuously visiting her for just over two years now, I have really come to enjoy my times with her. Plus, with her different health issues and medical ailments which disables her from getting out and socializing, I know it brightens her day that someone else is thinking of her and wants to spend time with her.

Honour others. We had guest ministry come to church one weekend. She had preached about storms and how certain trees were meant to weather the storm. She then asked people to come up who were going through a storm so that she could pray for them. At that time, my parents had just divorced. I was in the middle of a storm. She came over and prayed for me. She began to speak prophetically over me that I was trying to fix everything in my family. Right there, I began to just sob. She was right, I had convinced myself that I was my family's savior. She told me that she felt God say that it's time to drop everything and to look to him for my help. God was the one who was going to fix my family, not me.

In the midst of me taking on the role of savior, I began to judge my family for acting the way they did. I began to dishonor them in my words I used towards them. God showed me that everyone grieves in their own way, and that their grieving process may look different from mine. My brothers, my mother and father, and myself were all grieving the loss of our former family unit, and that was okay. God showed me that even more in this season that I need to extend grace to my family and continue to honor them despite how they were acting.

Where there was once strength there was now dysfunction. No family is perfect, and God has been teaching me how to honor other's feelings, attitudes and decisions. To this day I still don't know why my father left my mother, or why my parents actually got a divorce, but they are still my parents, and through God's grace I am learning how to honor them.

Now I know in the Bible God says that we need to honour our mother and father. Ways that we do that are: submitting to them, listening to them, not back talking, doing what they ask of us, not putting them down or disrespecting them. So, we honour our parents through our words and actions.

Exodus 20:12 says, *"Honour your father and mother. Then you will live a long, full life in the land the LORD your God is giving you."* (NLT) It's the first command that God gave Moses of the ten commandments and it's the only one with a promise attached to it. Simply, if I honour my parents, God promises that I will live a long, full life. I mean who doesn't want that, right?

Since my parents' divorce, there has been an area of weakness for me. The thoughts and words that I have had for my parents have not been honourable. I judged them and I looked down on them. I was certainly not on the track to reaping any rewards in my future with the way I was acting. I found it hard to respect two people who I believe just gave up on our family- at least that's what I thought. I now know that there are always two sides to a story. I found it hard to respect people who were acting so immature. Their divorce became petty, and I had a really hard time with having a good attitude towards them. My parents were not used to being on their own so they held on to their relationships with us. And as adult children that caught my brother's and I off guard. It didn't help that my brothers would verbally dishonor my parents and I would just go along with it.

God had to get a hold of me, because I was out of control when it came dishonouring my parents. God showed me that no matter how my parents were acting, that they were both hurting and that I was to honour them by speaking life over them and speaking respectfully of them. Even if my parents were wrong in the way they talked negatively about each other, I had to honour them. This was hard for me to grasp, and I'm not perfect, but I aim each day to honour my parents in what I say and do. So, let's be children that set the trend of honouring our parents even in the face of adversity.

Authority

I don't have any cute anecdotes or stories to tell you regarding this area of relationship in my life, but I have learned a lot over the last few years about authority and how we should treat those in positions of authority over us. I would like to pass on my gained knowledge to you in the hopes that you will learn from my mistakes.

Authority is defined as: "the power to give orders or make decisions: the power or right to direct or control someone or something."[xvi] The purpose of authority is to create boundaries for us that allow us to live safely. An example of this is the law. Police officers work to enforce the law to citizens for our good, not theirs. The law has been put in place to stop us from getting hurt. If we run a red light we could get into a car accident so we obey the law that says to stop at a red light.

Due to the strained relationship with my mom, I had a hard time with authority in general. I never really appreciated authority figures because I did not believe that they truly had my best interest at heart. I would constantly challenge them, refusing to do what they told me to do. I did not like to be controlled, and as a young girl I only saw authority for the purpose of controlling so I didn't like authority. One day when I finally came to the Lord, he opened me up to being able to trust in authority figures again. Through a slow process of being able to learn from, be guided by and unconditionally loved by God I started to see the benefits of authority figures in my life.

WHAT I LEARNED

Authority is God appointed. When I came to faith I quickly learned that God created authority for a reason and that we were supposed to respect them. Romans 13:1 plainly says "For all authority comes from God, and those in positions of authority have been placed there by God." Any authority figures in our life, whether we disagree with them or not, have all been appointed by God. God put them there for a reason.

Submit to authority. There are different types of authorities in our lives. God is number one, we must first and foremost always respect and reverently fear the Lord and His lordship. Other authority figures in our lives are: teachers, police officers, government officials (Prime Minister, Chancellors, Counsellors, etc.), pastors, parents, mentors, grandparents, our bosses, etc. We have plenty of opportunities to learn to submit to authority.

Daniel was under the rule of King Nebuchadnezzar, who was not a Christian and even erected a statue of himself where he forced people to worship and forced the Israelites to stop worshipping God. He was not a good leader/authority, but Daniel submitted to a point. (Daniel 3) That's another point to make, yes, we are meant to submit to all authority, but if that authority is going against our fundamental belief/faith system and making us do something we know goes against the ultimate authority (God); we need to take a stand for what we believe in.

Every time I find myself disagreeing with something my boss is doing or something that our government does, I just remind myself of Romans 13:1, *"all authority is God appointed"* and we must respect them. And we should always strive to honour them. John Bevere wrote this great book called Honor's Reward. It "unveils the powerful truth of an often-overlooked principle: the spiritual law of honour. If you understand and practice this virtue, you will attract blessing both now and for eternity."[xvii] God calls us to honour those leaders/authority figures in our lives even the harsh ones. We honour them by submitting to their authority, not bad talking them, but by doing what they tell us to do so long as it does not go against our morals and praying and interceding for them on a regular basis even when we don't feel like it.

Pray for authority. This is something I started implementing on a daily basis- praying and interceding for those authority figures in my life: my parents, government officials, bosses, pastors, etc. By doing this my view of authority shifted. If this is an area that your struggle with I invite you to begin to pray for the authority in your life even if you aren't in agreement with them, lift them up to God and watch him change the way you think about them.

Friendships

I've had an interesting past when it comes to friendships in my life. I formed some not-so-healthy habits along the way and have learned many lessons. When I was a little girl my mother didn't really allow us to go over the other children's houses to just "hang out." We hung out with cousins and friends of the family. So, although I did have a good set of friends in elementary school, I wasn't as close with them because I didn't get to see them outside of school very much.

I called those the wonder years, everyone was friends with everyone in my class. The whole class was invited to birthday parties- no one was ever left out. It was great. I got along with people so well. However, looking back at it now I see a scared little girl who desperately wanted to fit so she said the right things, pretended to like them.

Then flip the switch, I can't recall the exact moment when that happened, but I just remember feeling that I wanted to be different. I didn't care what people thought of me anymore. Because of my new-found attitude, I lost some friend. At around that same time a new girl started going to my school, her name was Christine. She was cool, edgy and didn't care what people thought of her. I became like her and stopped caring what people thought of me.

Then I moved schools in Grade 7, and my friend count started to dwindle. I did have friends, but it wasn't like before- it wasn't like everyone in my class was my friend. I didn't get invited to any parties. The friends I did have just wanted to use what I said to them, against me and gossip to whole school.

The summer before Grade 8, I met Lisa. Lisa was the older sister of a boy my younger brother would hang out with. They lived right across the street from us so I always saw Lisa but didn't really talk to her. One day my mom was talking with her mom telling her that we were going to be going to the same school as her in the fall. Yes, we moved schools again. Lisa and I started talking and realized we had a lot in common and became really good friends. She was my first best friend.

I am a year older than her so I moved onto high school before she did. Although we were in different schools we still became very close. We would hang out all the time. We got to know each other's families very well, and were always over at each other's houses. I enjoyed spending time with her and I am still friends with her to this day. I even had the privilege of being her maid of honour in her wedding. It's the only relationship that was formed from when I was young and is still going strong today. That is mainly because of her. She texts me, calls me and emails me when she doesn't hear from me for a while. I'm painting a very bleak picture of friendships in my past, but it wasn't until I started attending church on a regular basis and came to faith that I experienced what true friendship felt like.

WHAT I LEARNED

There are three main ways that I have learned over the years of how maintain purity within my friendships:

Selflessness: Philippians 2:4 states, *"Don't look out only for your own interests, but take an interest in others, too."* (NLT) Let's face it, it's human nature to be selfish. This is something I really had to learn. When I decided to start putting the needs of my friends above mine, I realize they were meeting my needs and my friendships were being nurtured.

Serve others: This is simple. I realized when I decided to start serving my friends, whether it was babysitting for them just because or helping them financially when they were in a bind, those friends tended to be more thankful and I was closer with them. There is something about serving one another that enriches our friendships. Let's look to Jesus who gave us the greatest example of this. He chose to leave His divinity in Heaven to come to earth and serve in the ultimate sacrifice of himself for us. Jesus says to His disciples in Matthew 20:28: *"For even the Son of Man came not to be served but to serve others."* (NLT) So, let's be like Jesus and serve our friends more! Is there something you can do right now in one of your friendships to serve them better?

Humility: Paul urges the Philippian church: "Don't do anything only to get ahead. Don't do it because you are proud. Instead, be humble. Value others more than yourselves. None of you should look out just for your own good. Each of you should also look out for the good of others." (Philippians 2:3-4, NIRV) When you have an attitude of putting others ahead of yourself, God honours that heart. The times I have decided to not schedule something in knowing a friend of mine might need me, or offer my babysitting services although I have had an extra-long week just so my friend and her husband can go out together alone have been some of the most rewarding moments of my life. Not only have I put their needs first, but I have showed them I love them by putting them first.

Ultimately God wants us all to have lively, healthy relationships and that takes work from both parties involved. It also takes letting God into our relationships. When we do this, He slowly begins to change our hearts to look like His and that's when we begin to operate in purity.

CHAPTER 4: PURITY IN MIND

Lustful Thoughts

When I first came to Christ I had a secret sin that I struggled with for almost three years before Jesus finally set me free from it once and for all. That sin was lustful thoughts. I would know that they were wrong to entertain but felt powerless to stop them.

In order to understand why lustful thoughts are such a big deal and create impurity in our lives, we need to explore God's plan for sex. God created us with sexual desires for a reason, to *"reproduce and fill the earth!"* (Genesis 1:26-27, MSG) God created us so that we can fill the earth by procreation. How do achieve that? Well through the act of what the Bible terms as *"becoming one flesh."* (Genesis 2:24, MSG) Therefore we can conclude from this that we need to have sexual desires in order for us to fulfill our main purpose on this earth.

Unfortunately, when Adam and Eve sinned in the garden, they opened the door up to sin in our lives (better termed as the "fall of man"). As more humans were born they were automatically born into sin. So, sin was no longer something we knew not of, but it became our nature. And through this process, the pure and holy purpose of our sexual desires were twisted and perverted, by Satan's influence I believe, and lust was born to man. The dictionary defines lust as "a very strong sexual desire."[xviii] Therefore, by this definition, lustful thoughts are simply thoughts attached to a very strong sexual desire.

What is interesting about lust is that it is not something new- it always existed. The Old Testament of the Bible is full of all types of sins. God even gives Moses, hundreds of generations after Adam and Eve, a bunch of laws of what not to do based on the sins that were already being committed. Lust falls into the category of sexual immorality- those earthly desires, which we are meant to avoid. (Colossians 3:5, ESV) It is not something new. Sounds depressing, right? Well there is good news, but before I tell you that let's take a look at how God so meticulously crafted us for procreation.

We are all born with sexual desires. However, normally they are not awakened in us until the stage of puberty. The years leading up to and during puberty are when the body starts to become sexually mature.

Let's go on a little anatomy lesson of puberty where we will start with a hormone called gonadotrophin- releasing hormone (GNRH), which is released in the brain. When it reaches the pituitary gland in the body, two more hormones are released: luteinizing hormone (LH) and follicle-stimulating hormone (FSH). Both these hormones manifest in the body in different ways, also depending on if you are male or female. One of the main ways we notice a change is in an awakening of our sexual desires.

In order to understand how the door to lust was opened in my life we have to go back to beginning, when I was the precious age of two. I was sexually molested by someone I knew very well. It happened again at the age of five from someone different and then again at the age of nine by yet another person. All three men I knew well and I trusted them.

Because of what happened to me, I had a developed a strong sexual desire as a child that was only increased when I began to go through puberty. That desire turned into lust and I found myself having constant lustful thoughts. Solomon's lover in Songs of Solomon 3:5 warn us, *"Don't excite love, don't stir it up, until the time is ripe- and you're ready."* (MSG) The word for love in this verse is *"ahabah"* in Hebrew, which literally translates to "love sick." Solomon's lover is warning the women of the village to not awaken our "love sickness" until the time is right.

Like God's command in Genesis, sexual desire is meant to be awakened in the right circumstances. *"That's why a man leaves his father and mother and is joined to his wife. The two of them become one."* (Genesis 2:24, ERV) Therefore, sexual desire is awakened within the confines of marriage- those are the right circumstances; the right timing. That way you and your spouse can fulfill God's original plan within the boundaries of marriage. When a desire is awakened outside of its proper circumstances, it can easily lead to sin in your life.

King Solomon warns us in Song of Songs 3:5 where he says this: *"Promise me, O women of Jerusalem, by the gazelles and wild deer, not to awaken love until the time is right."* (NLT) Gods intention for us was to never awaken love until the time was right; until we were married. It's only in that right timing of marriage can the true purpose for sexual desire be fulfilled and satisfied. It's a safe place for it and as a matter of fact should be the only place for it.

My "awakening" led to a hidden sin. That's the thing with sin, we tend to hide it from others because we are usually ashamed of it. Adam and Eve hid from God when they realized that they did something wrong (sin) because they were ashamed (Genesis 3). I didn't like the sin I was committing, but I was hooked and I felt like I couldn't stop it. The thrill that I could get caught, the instant gratification from it felt great! But like all things that bring us instant gratification, there is usually sacrifice and long-term consequences. For me the sacrifice was my freedom, and the long-term consequence was the stronghold of lustful thoughts in my life- that feeling that made me think I couldn't stop.

WHAT I LEARNED

When I had decided to do the No More GAGA program, I was knee deep in lustful thoughts. They would pop up at the most unpredictable times. The first thing that this program addressed with me were those lustful thoughts. GAGA gave me a way out. Remember this: You will never be tempted beyond anything you can't handle and when you are tempted God will always give you a way out. (1 Corinthians 10:13)

Some things I learned about lust on my journey to freedom:

Lust is a choice. The Bible defines lust as "a strong craving or desire, often of a sexual nature."[xix] So lust is an emotion usually coupled by thoughts and actions. The Oxford dictionary defines an emotion as an "instinctive or intuitive feeling as distinguished from reasoning or knowledge."[xx] So an emotion is a very physical response like we found out earlier in Chapter 2. The definition takes it one step further to say that an emotion is a strong feeling. It's something you feel. And although it feels like you can't control it, it's still a choice. Like any temptation, you can say no, but it takes willingness and strategy and most importantly the Holy Spirit. I'm living proof of that. I know what it feels like to think you are trapped and that there is no way out, but in most cases, you probably haven't tapped into the God given power to break free from that temptation. God promises a way out and His Word is something we can stand on.

It took me a while to grasp this concept. I thought, *"You mean all I have to do is say no to lust and the thoughts will go away?"* Well it's not that simple. Saying no to lust meant saying no to anything that triggered lustful thoughts: music, movies, books, magazines, paintings, etc. It meant saying no to people that I lusted after, removing those images from my home or stop hanging around certain men. I had to literally starve my sexual desires of triggers that caused those lustful thoughts. It's not an easy process, but I started to see results immediately after I purged my life of objects that elicited lustful thoughts. The thoughts started to diminish, but I still struggled.

Shine a Light. It's not until we take the brave step of admitting our sin to someone else or even God, that the sin begins to lose its power and grip over our lives. Secret sin derives its power from remaining a secret. That way the enemy can keep us trapped in shame, embarrassment, confusion and worthlessness. Through this sin Satan attacks our identity and isolates us so we won't tell anyone and stay in our prison of fear of not being accepted. Mark 4:22 states *"What is hidden is meant to be seen. And what is put out of sight is meant to be brought out into the open."* (NIRV) God does not want us to live in secret. He wants us to be open with each other.

James urges us to confess our sins to one another. (James 5:16) Something happens when we begin to confess our sins to one another and bring to the light what was once in the dark. We don't feel isolated anymore and we are able to use the wisdom and knowledge of those around us to help us overcome that sin. We are able to lean on each other to help each other grow strong again. I encourage you, that if you are struggling with a secret sin to confess it to someone you trust- wise counsel. Someone who may have gone through something similar or the exact same thing? They could even be your way out, sent by God like the GAGA program was for me.

Go to the Word. The Bible is filled with information, strategy and practical tips for our everyday lives. If you're not getting into the Word every day I challenge to begin doing so. This single-handedly changed my life for the better. Every day I read my Bible, and it is full of answers to questions I have, especially when I have to decide. It's all right there. The Bible has a lot to say about lust:

1. *Have nothing to do with it. "So put to death the sinful, earthly things lurking within you. Have nothing to do with sexual immorality, impurity, lust, and evil desires."* (Colossians 3:5, NLT) That's pretty straight forward. Remove lust from your life.

2. *Don't follow your sinful nature: "When you follow the desires of your sinful nature, the results are very clear: sexual immorality, impurity, lustful pleasures, idolatry, sorcery, hostility, quarrelling, jealousy, outbursts of anger, selfish ambition, dissension, division, envy, drunkenness, wild parties, and other sins like these. Let me tell you again, as I have before, that anyone living that sort of life will not inherit the Kingdom of God."* (Galatians 5:19, NLT) Stay away from your sinful nature as it only leads to strongholds of sin in your life.

3. *Run from it: "Run from anything that stimulates youthful lusts."* (2 Timothy 2:22, NLT) Run, run, fun from lust. When you see anything in your life that will lead to lust or you are placed in situations, physically run away from them. The Bible is clear on this.

4. *Keep far away from it. "Keep far away from sexual sins. All the other sins a person commits are outside the body. But sexual sins are sins against their own body."* (1 Corinthians 6:18, NLT) Keep away from lust as it's a sexual sin that is against your body, which is meant to be the temple of the Holy Spirit.

For the most part in the Bible, lust is talked about in terms of warning. Paul warns the different churches to stay away, have nothing to do with and fully abstain from sexual sins (lust). Go ahead do your own Bible study on what it says about lust. Learn why it is such a strong sin and such a common sin. Let God's Word guide you into all knowledge and wisdom.

Expect opposition. I remember when I got to that point in my life where I was ready to be done with lustful thoughts once and for all. I had enough with the old pattern of overcoming and falling right back into it again. I knew it wasn't easy and it was going to take me doing something I never did before. Because how many of us know that in order to achieve something new we have to be willing to do something we've never done before?

I had recently overcome this area of my life through accountability, prayer, and the Word of God. That day I had thoughts bombarding me like never before. I couldn't look at a man without thinking things I should have never thought. I started to think that something was wrong with me and that I would never overcome this area of my life. So, I decided to fight back!

Know that when you begin to gain freedom in any area of your life, you will get opposition. I remember when I first started working through my freedom from lustful thoughts. Two weeks into it those thoughts came steamrolling back into my mind. This is the only strategy from Satan to keep you where you're at. He doesn't want you to gain freedom. That's one less area of your life that he will have control over. The enemy is very possessive. Watch out! Paul puts it plainly, *"Your enemy the devil is like a roaring lion. He prowls around looking for someone to chew up and swallow."* (1 Peter 5:8, NIRV) The enemy is seeking for any way to get you down and keep you down. Don't expect that he will just lie down and allow you to gain back your freedom. You have to fight for it. I remember times when I would recite the same verse over and over and over until it became my reality. There were times when it would stick in my head and other times I would have to repeat that Scripture until my thoughts changed.

Also know this, the battle has already been won! You are victorious through Christ Jesus! Notice how I said that in the present tense? Whatever you are facing today you already have the victory over it through Christ. The enemy has lost. Don't let him intimidate you into thinking otherwise.

There is a way out. We already know that there is no temptation too great for us- God has already given us a way out of it. All we have to do is seek God and ask him for strategy and His power to overcome. My strategy came in the form of the GAGA program. After we prayed, I looked up what the Bible had to say about lust and then began to declare Scriptures over my life of what I wanted to see:

2 Corinthians 10:4-5 states: *"The weapons we fight with are not the weapons of the world. On the contrary, they have divine power to demolish strongholds. We demolish arguments and every pretension that sets itself up against the knowledge of God, and we take captive every thought to make it obedient to Christ."* (NLT) What I took away from this Scripture was:

1. *God has given me weapons to fight with:*

    a. *The Word of God.* The sword of the Spirit (Ephesians 6:17), and sharper than a double-edged sword (Hebrews 4:12). We are meant to put on the belt buckle of truth (Hebrews 4:11), the truth is found in the Word of God.

    b. *Praise and worship.* The Israelites saw firsthand how the walls of Jericho fell at the sound of their praise (Joshua 6:20).

    c. *Prayer.* Even Jesus said to the disciples when they couldn't drive out a demon from someone. *"This kind can come out only by prayer."* (Mark 9:29, NIRV) Sometimes in order to overcome the hold the enemy has over your life you just to get before God and pray.

2. *Those weapons have power to demolish:*

    a. *Strongholds.* The Greek word for stronghold is *ochuróma*, which means: "anything on which one relies." It comes from the root "oxyroo" which means to fortify. As in a military stronghold or strong fortress.[xxi] That is how strong a stronghold is. It's a sin that takes shelter inside of you making you think it is part of who you are. But God promises that there is a way out, because the weapons He has given us help us to demolish strongholds. Suffer from constant negative thinking? Or lustful thoughts, like I did? Just use the weapon of praise, when your thoughts are so focused on God, they can't be focused on anything else.

b. *Arguments.* (how does this relate to lust?) Arguments are any opinion that negates the truth of God. Paul warns his brother Titus to: *"... stay away from those who have foolish arguments and talk about useless family histories and argue and quarrel about the law. Those things are worth nothing and will not help anyone."* (Titus 3:9, NLT) Through the Word of God that tells us to stay away from such arguments, we are able to destroy any argument that comes our way. How can someone argue when no one is there to argue with them? I encourage you to try that the next time someone begins an argument with you.

c. *Pretension.* A pretense is "an attempt to make something that is not the case appear true."[xxii] So a pretension is an effort to establish that which is not true as true. That's an easy one. When faced with a lie or that which wants to be true but is really a lie, put it test to the Word. Does what their saying line up with the Word of God? If not, then right there through the weapon of the Word of God you have demolished that pretension.

3. *I can take every thought captive and make it obedient to Christ:*

a. *Make thoughts obedient to Christ.* This means that those thoughts that don't align with the truth, you have been given authority to realign with the truth. So how we do that?

For me, I struggled with lustful thoughts that would pop up at any time, sometimes at the most inconvenient times. They would make me lose my concentration, distract me or throw me for a loop. My weapon for those thoughts was the Word of God. I encourage you to ask God for a Scripture that you can use to fight back whatever adverse thoughts you struggle with. 2 Corinthians 10:4-5 was my go-to Scripture. I wrote it down on a cue card, and personalized it like this:

The weapons of our warfare are not of this, but are mighty in God for the pulling down to strongholds. I pulled down arguments and every high and lofty thought that raises itself against the knowledge of God. And I take every thought captive to obey Christ. (NLT)

When that lustful thought would pop into my head, I would start to speak this Scripture out loud. Be warned that just because you declare a Scripture here and there, those thoughts are not just going to go away. The enemy is not willing to give up the territory he has in your life. You need to fight for it. That's why we have weapons, for the battle. Sometimes, I would have to repeat that Scripture 10- 15 times until my thoughts were rerouted. I even had times when I went days, weeks and even months without any lustful thoughts. Then boom, out of the blue, they would come rushing back into my head. I seriously thought that I would never get free from this area of my life. As I consistently was diligent in speaking that Scripture over my mind, it finally came into line with the Word of God and I was set free once and for all.

Take every thought captive. It says right in the Bible that God has given us weapons to take every thought captive that does not line up with His truth. How do we do that, and what does it look like?

This is simply done by being aware of what you are thinking. When are aware, you can catch the thoughts that you shouldn't be thinking, and literally take them captive by choosing not to entertain them. So today, I can say with confidence that I am completely free from lustful thoughts. That doesn't stop the enemy from trying his old tricks. Now I simply become aware of the thought and choose not to entertain it.

Identify triggers. For me watching certain movies, seeing certain images, even watching scenes in movies would trigger lustful thoughts. The only reason why lustful thoughts became a stronghold in my life was that I was feeding it. I was giving it what it needed to survive and grow stronger. If you starve it, it will die sooner or later. So that's what I did, I had to give up those romantic comedy (Rom Coms) movies.

Now I know what you're saying, "Rom Coms are all I watch, what else would I watch?" This was not easy for me, but I was desperate for freedom so I was willing to do whatever it took. So, I cut out watching all Rom Coms. At first, I replaced those rom coms with actions films, which then I realized had certain scenes in them that I had no business watching. You know the scenes I'm talking about! (In case you don't know, the no go zone for me were the kissing scenes in movies and tv shows.) I was at a point where I couldn't even watch the kissing scenes in movies. I still don't to this day. I don't want to go back to where I was before, so I still choose not to watch the kissing scenes in movies. Sounds a bit extreme, but as I heard before "I am always a thought away from going back to where I used to be." (Anonymous) I don't want to recreate a stronghold that I worked so hard to be set free from. What's the point? Remember in order to get different results, you have to be willing to do something you have never done before. Trust me, I tried watching the odd kissing scene here and there, and I knew right away that I shouldn't had done that. As you walk with God, He will give you wisdom on what to watch and what not to watch. Plus, the Holy Spirit will convict you in all right living.

I even went as far as giving up looking at magazines with male models in them. This is how committed I was. I mean if the devil is relentlessly pursuing me to see if I would mess up, then I had to be just as ruthless in pursuing my freedom. You won't overcome strongholds in your life by being idle. Get serious, get motivated and get a plan.

Purging items. Part of the GAGA program right at the beginning was that we would have to purge those items in our life that would not help us in completing the program. For me that included all secular music, romantic novels, posters of male models, any paraphernalia from ex-boyfriends, and romantic comedy DVDs. This was serious, and so was I. I know I am repeating myself, but when you have an adversary who is willing to stop at nothing to make you fail and is just looking for an opportunity to take you down, you need to become serious. To this day, years later I still do not have those items in my life. This was the second main component to why I am free today. Are there items in your life, that are keeping you from your freedom? Why not try purging them for a set period, and see what God does in your life. Maybe for you its deleting an ex's phone number from your phone, or maybe getting rid of old photos, putting down the magazines, not watching romantic movies like me, or maybe choosing not to watch porn? Whatever it is for you, my prayer is that you would have the strength to be able to purge those items necessary for your freedom.

Lustful thoughts are no joke and if we struggle with them we should stop at nothing to remove them from our lives. They are just polluting them. I am praying for you if this is an area of struggle for you. As you embark on your journey to overcome this area of your life it is my prayer that God would give you wisdom and strength to be more than conqueror! He's got you and you've got this is!

Negative thoughts

When I turned 13 a switch went off in my brain. I can't explain it. All of sudden I was riddled with anxious, depressive, negative and suicidal thoughts. I felt like I was going crazy.

I remember it like it was yesterday. I was sitting down in church and the priest was talking about Jesus dying on the cross and how He rose again and that when we believe in Christ we too will die and go to heaven one day. Something snapped in me, and anxious thoughts about death and dying bombarded my head. I started crying, and not just tears gently running down your cheeks. I started to cry out loud with big sobs and gestures. My dad had to quickly usher me out of mass to the back of the church to calm me down. It took a while, because I remember not going back in to service that morning. I remember being so afraid of dying and there being nothing after death.

In this church I served as an altar girl. So I would love doing weddings and funerals as I would normally get paid. Soon after this attack (that is what I am calling it, as to this day I am not sure what happened), I stopped volunteering for funerals, as the mere mention of death would send my thoughts swirling into a frenzy of doubt, fear and extreme anxiety. This later on lead to many panic attacks through the years to come for me, and eventually into depression.

In ninth grade, the book we were reading in English class was The Chrysalids. For those of you who have not heard about this book, it was written by a British author by the name of John Wyndham. The book is about a boy named David who lives in "a tight-knit community of religious and genetic fundamentalists, who exist in a state of constant alert for any deviation from what they perceive as the norm of God's creation, deviations broadly classified as "offenses" and "blasphemies…" Offenses consist of plants and animals that are in any way unusual, and these are publicly burned to the accompaniment of the singing of hymns. Blasphemies are human beings—ones who show any sign of abnormality, however trivial. They are banished from human society, cast out to live in the wild country…"[xxiii]

You can just imagine a fourteen-year-old me who suffered from anxiety, depression and panic attacks reading a book about a world that survived an apocalypse. I read the first chapter and broke down into tears because it elicited such fear and thoughts about how there is nothing after death. Suffice to say my teacher ended up giving me a separate book to read from my peers. That's how much I was suffering.

My teenage years were hard, by the time I turned fifteen I didn't trust anyone. I thought everyone was against me and/or judging me. I was a bit of a loner in high school and did not have very many friends. Like I said before, those years were my dark ages. Negative thinking was the norm for me. I mean every time I would try to think positively, it would never go the way I wanted it to. So, I didn't bother thinking positively. I was an avid pessimist, but I masked it with statements that "I was being a realist." Deep down I knew the truth.

What's in a thought?

"Negative thinking is a thought process where people tend to find the worst in everything, or reduce their expectations by considering the worst possible scenarios."[xxiv] So a negative thought can look very different for everyone. For me there were three main themes that took the form of negative thoughts:

1. **My self-worth.** I had constant feelings of worthlessness and that I didn't measure up to people's expectations of me. I always thought I just wasn't good enough and I didn't deserve to have good things happen to me.

2. **Life after death.** I was plagued with anxiety and hopelessness that this was all the life we had and after we had died, that was the end of it all. I struggled to wrap my head around that concept, and always came up empty. These thoughts were the main reason of panic attacks for me.

3. **Others judging me.** I always just assumed that everyone was judging me, assuming the worst in me. This kept me at a distance from everyone in high school. Like I mentioned earlier, I isolated myself for fear of being judged.

Today I can look back, having learned what I know now, and say confidently that every single one of those negative thoughts were lies that I believed that came from my core beliefs. I truly believed all those things and therefore that's what I thought about most of the time. That is important to note, because as my belief system began to slowly change so did my thoughts and thinking patterns.

Negative thoughts plagued me badly. I'm not talking the occasional down day. I'm talking every day being depressed, fearful, and anxious- having zero peace. I know there are people just like me out there today suffering from negative thinking, wondering if they will overcome this area of their life. I am here to tell that YOU WILL, because I did!

WHAT I LEARNED

Truth for lies. We have already established that negative thoughts are lies that we are believing. So how do we overcome lies? Through truth: *"Then you will know the truth. And the truth will set you free."* (John 8:32, NIRV) Once we expose the truth of the lie we were believing we change that negative thought into a positive thought.

I once learned a method for overcoming negative thoughts. I would renounce the lie I was believing, ask God to show me the spiritual root of that lie and then ask him to show me the truth. It's that simple. For example:

Lie: There is no life after death.
Root: Fear of dying.
Truth: John 3:16 states, *"God so loved the world that he gave his one and only Son. Anyone who believes in him will not die but will have eternal life."* (NIRV)

This process literally changed my thoughts, because how many of us know that when we change our thoughts we change our life?

Another example:
Lie: I am worthless.
Root: Being rejected.
Truth: Jeremiah 29:11 states *""For I know the plans I have for you," says the Lord. "Plans for good and not for disaster. Plans to give you a future and a hope."* (NIVUK) I read that as I have a purpose to fulfill on this earth, so if I was worthless why would God have a plan for my life?

Now it's your turn. You try it. Are there negative thoughts plaguing your mind? Can't seem to shake them loose? Ask God to show you the truth for the lies you are believing. I will be praying for you friends, that you will find peace in your mind and love in your hearts as you work towards gaining freedom in this area of your life. Remember, negative thoughts do not come from God, so get ready to fight using the divine weapons you have been given.

Overcome the minefield in order to embrace the battlefield. This notion of minefield of the mind came to me one week as I was feeling bombarded by negative thoughts. Picture this, a soldier is walking through a minefield. They are trying to be extra careful, because they could set off a bomb at any time. Sometimes, I felt like negative thoughts were constantly crowding my head, taking over my thought life. I felt like I couldn't think without having a negative thought. Like that minefield, I just didn't know what was going to set it off.

In the song "Standard" by the Planetshakers, there is a line that says "when the enemy comes like a flood..." How many of us know that when the enemy attacks, he comes from all sorts of angles? He is looking to steal, kill and destroy us. This type of thinking is giving in to the enemy and the thoughts he is placing in our minds or the negative thoughts we are focusing on. We don't have to accept this notion of minefield of the mind or ever feel like we are in an actual minefield in our minds, because we have already been given the victory through Christ Jesus. Sometimes the enemy wants us to think we are in a minefield but in fact we are in a battlefield.

Joyce Meyer wrote a book about the battlefield, called "Battlefield of the Mind." In it she goes through all the tactics the enemy uses to attack us and the battlefield he chooses is our mind. *"For as he thinks in his heart, so is he."* (Proverbs 23:7, NKJV) This is basically saying that we are what we think. If Satan wants to get us at the core of who we are, where does he attack? Our minds. It's also one of our weak spots because from there can spring all sorts of evil and no one would ever know, because it's on the inside of us.

You see this notion of battlefield of the mind is very different from minefield of the mind. With a minefield we don't have an advantage. Anything can set off a negative thought. However, with the battlefield of the mind we have a fighting chance. Like any battle we can prepare, we can put up boundaries, and we can wield our weapons to fight back. And we already know that we have been given weapons to fight with.

One of those weapons are called "battle cries." Simply put, a battle cry is a statement of truth that negates any lies you are believing. Normally negative thoughts stem from lies. We already know that combat lies with truth. Battle cries are those statements of truth we decide to speak over our life when we feel attacked. Or in the heat of the moment you might find yourself actually crying out the truth in the face of the enemy to let him know that you already have the victory!

As I end this chapter, it is my hope that you have been given tools to help you fight the battle. And that when you find yourself knee deep in negative thoughts that you will stand and realize that you already know the tactics of the enemy. You can fight back, and have been given weapons of mass destruction to do that with. The victory has already been won. So as you embrace your battlefields and choose to fight, remember that you are not alone. God says, *"the battle is not yours."* (2 Chronicles 20:15, NLT) It belongs to him and all he asks is that we fight with him. With our eyes focused on him we can win any battle. I can't wait to hear your battle stories.

CHAPTER 5: PURITY IN WAITING

What are we doing in the waiting periods of our lives; what are we actually waiting for? A perfect man/woman to come along, that perfect job, that perfect opportunity to serve God, that perfect situation in which we can reach out to someone? *What are we waiting for?* The Bible describes waiting as staying in a place of expectation in your heart. The verb *waiting* is a transitive verb, which means it involves acting. It's mustering the strength to stand still although we are in expectation of something that hasn't happened in our lives yet. In this season of us standing still and learning to wait we are guarding our hearts and focusing on God.

In order for us to truly know what purity in waiting looks like we need to look at how we wait well in the waiting period. Once we overcome discouragement, controlling our own timeline, impatience, doubt and fears about God coming through in our lives then we can truly begin to wait well. I will be talking about that later on in this chapter.

Sometimes we get impatient and want to try to make things happen in our own strength, but God calls us to wait on him. Psalm 62:5 gives us a perfect example of what we should be doing in the season of waiting: *"Let all that I am wait quietly before God, for my hope is in him."* (NLT) Wait for God in all that we are: wait for him in thought, in word, in heart and action:

Thoughts

We need to ensure our thoughts are pure during our period of waiting. Are we anxious, doubtful that God won't do what He has promised? Are we impatient and already thinking of ways to get what we want in our own efforts? Isaiah 30:15 says *"In quietness and confidence is your strength."* (NLT) Do we quiet our minds to focus on God? Because it is only when we quiet our minds before God, that He can talk to us and we can hear from him. We can receive wisdom and discernment in any situation we are in. His promise is that we will never give us more than we can handle. He gives us a way out- a way to live through the waiting. (1 Corinthians 10:13)

Actions

How are our actions in the waiting period? God tells us exactly what we should be doing in the waiting: *"Be still, and know that I am God!"* (Psalm 46:10, NLT) So God is actually asking us to make sure our actions are aligning with two things: standing still, and not striving to make things happen in our own strength.

There is a couple in my church who were waiting for children. They had a promise from God that they were going to have many children but it had been a couple years into their marriage and still no child. As they looked to God they felt the Holy Spirit lead them to start calling each other as "mother" and "father" as a prophetic action to speak into existence that which is not. They began to act as parents before He actually gave them children. Now they have four beautiful children. Their actions were in line with God's promises during the waiting period. God wants us to focus on him and truly to get to know him in our time of waiting. Get to know God's nature, His character, so that we can wait confidently on who God is and the fact that He always fulfills His promises. We are shifting our minds towards "the Person of our faith and away from the object of our wait." (*Wait and See*, p.107)

Words

Do our words have confidence that God will come through and that He will do what He promises in our lives? Do we allow the length of our waiting period to change our words? I don't know about you, but this was a big weakness for me. I would speak what I saw in the natural, although I wanted the opposite to be true.

What words are we speaking over our waiting period? During my church's 40-day negativity fast, we all committed to speaking life over areas of our lives. God gave me a revelation during this time of the words I was speaking over the men in my church; especially the single men. Whenever someone would ask me about the single men in my church, I would always respond with the standard "there are no good men in my church." I was speaking death, not life over the men in my church. So God encouraged me to invest 21 days in focused prayer over the men of my church. Instead of focusing on the lack, pray for the blessing.

As I did this, I noticed my attitude changed towards the men in my church. I had a new-found respect for them and I was able to interact with them in love. Before that I would avoid men and always think the worst of them. I shifted my focus and ended up with a renewed mind. It is important that our words are speaking life over our waiting periods. Psalm 141:3 states *"Set a guard, O Lord, over my mouth; keep watch over the door of my lips."* (NKJV) Words are very powerful- *"death and life are in the power of the tongue."* (Proverbs 18:21, NKJVs) Are we speaking life in our times of waiting or allowing the enemy to influence our words into speaking death? Are we allowing God to guard our lips so that we only speak life? We must be careful in what we are saying in these times of waiting. If we don't we could end up delaying the object of our wait and extending our waiting period.

Heart

Lastly, what are our motives in waiting? Why do we want what we want? I know this an area I needed to be clear in. I needed to get my heart and motives in check when it came to wanting marriage. I remember when God challenged me with this question. At first, I had no idea how to answer it. As I got closer to God my answer for this question changed and took shape. A few years ago the reason why I wanted to get married was to have a life partner, someone that I can do stuff with. More recently I would have answered it with "because I want to have children." Probably not the best of motives, but it was practical. Now I realize that my future marriage is not just about me. It is all about fulfilling God's purpose for our marriage.

God has a plan, not only for my life, but also for my marriage which is part of my life. He has a purpose that only my husband and I can fulfill. What are our motives? Proverbs 16:2 states *"People may be pure in their own eyes, but the Lord examines their motives."* (NLT) God knows our heart and what is in it. So are our motives pure in the waiting period? Are we waiting for the right reasons? Allow God to reveal His will in our waiting.

As a single woman, it sometimes gets difficult to silence the deep desire that God has placed within me, and I really don't believe God wants me to silence it. I believe God has given me that desire to get married and have children. It has been His plan for most of us (some are truly not called to this life), all along; since the day of Adam and Eve. *"It's not good for man to be alone."* (Genesis 2:18, NLT) That's not just His plan, but it's also His promise. As a woman of strong faith, I know well enough that if God promises me something, it will come to pass.

Sometimes, if you're anything like me, you could let lies into your heart that tell you that you aren't ever going to get married. I believed this lie for many years, even after God spoke specifically to me about this area that He had a mate for me. Fear rose up in my heart and I believed that lie. As the years went by, I started to think that maybe I wasn't going to get married. God also gave me a vision for my marriage, but I still struggled to believe it.

Quite plainly, I was believing that lie because my eyes were no longer fixed on God and the promise that He gave me but instead became fixed on my current situation that I was not even close to having a potential partner so it didn't seem like I would ever meet him.

"God is not a man that he should lie." (Numbers 33:19, NLT) He is truth, the words He speaks to us are truth and can be relied upon to happen. In that moment I allowed my circumstances to dictate my life and not God's Word or His character -- who He really is: kind, merciful, patient, faithful, love, promise keeper, provider, truthful and just (Psalm 145:8- ERV, Proverbs 30:5- GNTD, Philippians 4:19- ESV, John 17:17- GNTD, Deuteronomy 32:4- NLT).

He promised me through His Word in Genesis 2:18 that it is not good for me to be alone. This concept is taken further in verse 24, where it states: *"Therefore, a man shall leave his father and mother and be joined to his wife."* (Genesis 2:24, NKJV) God's plan for us (all those who are called to marriage) is to not be alone on this earth. If you have a deep desire to get married, God wants to fulfill His promise to you- to send you a helper in life. Don't grow weary my friends, in doing what is right, because at just the right moment we will reap a reward, if we don't give up! (Galatians 6:9)

WHAT I LEARNED

Killing doubt and exercising faith. You see the enemy is prowling around like a lion, looking to see what/who he can devour. (1 Peter 5:8, NLT) Jesus said in John 10:10 that *"the thief's purpose is to steal, kill and destroy."* (NLT) The enemy is prowling around looking for any chance he can get to steal our faith, kill our joy and destroy our hope. We are most vulnerable to the enemy in our periods of waiting.

The enemy is prowling around looking for any chance he can get to steal our faith, kill our joy and destroy our hope.

Romans 14:23 says, *"Whatever is not from faith is sin [whatever is done with doubt is sinful]."* (AMP) That means if you do something that you doubt is right you are sinning. We already know that doubt is a type of uncertainty, wherein faith does not exist. Since doubt is the absence of faith in the context of Romans 14:23, doubt is sin. We need to be careful when doubt starts creeping in to our thinking patterns. If Adam and Eve are any indication of the consequence of doubt, we need to stand guard over our minds and hearts, that this doesn't happen to us.

It's easy to not have confidence in what we don't see, because it's not manifested in the natural world. But God calls us to live by faith, and not by sight. (2 Corinthians 5:7) So we combat doubt with faith. Faith is the confidence in what we hope for will actually happen, it gives us assurance of things we cannot see. (Hebrews 11:1). God promises us a living hope that is consistently working on the inside of us. If we cling to this hope, it will anchor our souls so that we don't get tossed around by the winds of our thoughts. (James 1:6-8). So we need to put faith back in the equation.

Yes, my natural circumstances say that I am in my 30's and single plus I'm not getting any younger. Yes, there is currently no one in my life that I can see right now in the natural. But I will choose to live by faith that "I am ready," and that God has a hand- picked spouse out there just for me because God promised me already. As I wait, I cling to the hope God has freely given me and trust that my future husband is coming. So now when doubt comes, I can speak to those feelings "peace be still." God's got me, and is working all things for my good. (Romans 8:28)

Sometimes we can fall into the trap of doubt when we have waited for a long time and our natural circumstances don't look anything like the promise God has for our life. God wants us to know the truth that His plans of a hopeful future will come to pass (Jeremiah 29:11). If you are finding it hard to trust God, maybe it's time to come back to the source. He's our first love, and wants us to always remember that. He wants the best for us. And I believe that most of us have head knowledge of that truth, but very few of us have heart knowledge of that. God knows all and sees all. He knows our heart much better than we do- He created it and knit it together in our mother's womb. (Psalm 139:13-14) Don't you think He wants to fulfill the very desire that He placed within your heart? Since His character is truthful, our guarantee is that it if He placed a desire in our heart, it will come to pass, in our lives.

Sometimes we can forget God's character and who He is. God is a father, it's at the core of His very nature. Like a good father, He wants to protect us, teach us, shape us, mold us, love us, correct us, provide for us and spend time with us. Above of all, he wants a relationship with us. He wants all of us and He wants the best for us like any good father would want for their child. By that characteristic alone it should give us enough assurance that God wants to provide us with the best mate.

I mentioned earlier, God cannot lie. Are you reading this? GOD CANNOT LIE. This means that any promise or Word He has spoken is true and *will* come to pass. God's promise to Adam was that *"it is not good for the man to be alone."* (Genesis 2:18, NLT) That is His Word – His truth upon which we can stand. That means for those of us who are single, and have a desire in our heart for marriage- it will happen. By His Word alone we should be rejoicing!

In Genesis 2:18, God starts off by saying *"It is not good..."* Friends, you need to know that God is in the business of giving us good gifts. Therefore if His Word says "it is not good for man to be alone," then ultimately that is His plan for those of us who have the desire to get married. We need not doubt it, because we know God has a great plan for our lives. His Word promises us that it is not good for us to be alone, so He wants to give us the good- us being with someone else. He wants to give us a helper, a mate. Matthew 7:11 states, *"If you, then, though you are evil, know how to give good gifts to your children, how much more will your Father in heaven give good gifts to those who ask him."* (NIV) Jesus is comparing our earthly fathers who are evil compared to God wanting to give us good gifts, and how much more our Heavenly father who is perfect wants to give us good gifts. He wants to bring us a mate, a mate that will bless us beyond measure because that is His heart for you and me.

If you're still not convinced because, like me, you have been waiting a long while and as you get older, your prospects begin to dwindle in number, take heart in God's Word which states in James 1:17 that *"every good gift and every perfect gift is from above, and comes down from the Father of lights, with whom there is no variation or shadow of turning."* (NJKV) Let's focus on the last part of that verse: *"there is no variation or shadow of turning."* Another version puts it as *"he never changes or casts a shifting shadow."* (NLT) Simply put, the plan- good plan/promise that God has for our lives: to get married, has not changed. It was the same as when He first created us, the same as when He first spoke it to us and it still the same as we continue to wait for its fulfillment.

We can also stand on God's promise that all things work together for good to those who love God, and to those who are called according to His purpose. (Romans 8:28) This period of waiting is not meant to break us or wear us down. It's meant to prepare us, encourage us and shape us into the husband or wife we will someday be. This season of singleness is for our own good, it's part of God's overall purpose for our life: "to be fruitful and multiply." Just like Jesus had a season of preparation for His mission, so do we need a season of preparation for marriage called "singlehood."

The story of Ruth is a great example of someone who waited well. Boaz found her working and doing the Lord's work. She wasn't sitting on her rear-end dreaming about who her future husband would be. She was working in Boaz's fields providing food for her "family." (Ruth 1-2) How will your future spouse find you? Pining after a relationship or serving God and going about His business in your life? (A little tip my single friends: any man or woman of God is looking for someone who is hard working and focused- not lazy or idle. So if you don't know God's purpose for your life, I suggest you find it and start living it out in your life. I strongly believe that's where every future spouse should be found.)

Let me encourage you as you wait in this season to resist looking at it as a stepping-stone to the rest of your life. Singlehood is still very much a part of your life, sometimes a big part, and is a part of the purpose that God has for you. Life doesn't start at marriage. I say it starts now in our singleness when we have time to give our lives to Jesus in every arena. We have time and resources now to dedicate our whole lives to Jesus and the mission He has called each and every one of us to. Use this time, because we won't have it forever. Once we get married there are many other distractions that we must overcome to continue fulfilling God's purpose for our lives. It definitely is easier to start a ministry while single than when you're married. I'm not saying it's impossible to start a ministry when you're married, it's just brings with it its own set of challenges. Be used by God now, and I guarantee you He will keep you so busy that you won't even know when your future spouse walks into your life. It will all just happen. Keeping our eyes fixed firmly on God's way to maintain purity in this season.

Trust God. Another way we can stay pure in the season of waiting is through trusting God. I love the story of how David became King. King David trusted God, even before he became King. We see this small puny man kill Goliath, a mighty giant warrior that the whole Israelite army including King Saul was afraid of. David trusted in God. In Psalm 21:2 David is talking about a King who went to war and came back victorious: *"You have given him his heart's desire and have not withheld the request of his lips."* He goes on to say in verses four and seven: *"He asked life from You, and You gave it to him— For the king trusts in the LORD..."* (NKJV) But I believe that it was because the king trusted in God, like David did, that he stepped out in faith to fight and was victorious. In order for us to have great faith for our circumstances we need to increase our trust in God. Trusting God requires knowing God very intimately, and once you know God, it's easy to have faith in him for your situation.

So in order to trust God for our future marriages, we need to know who God is. When we really and truly know who God is, which comes from getting into His Word and seeking His presence daily, then faith becomes a by-product of that. This happens because of the trust we have built up in us towards God. So I encourage you that if you don't have an intimate relationship with God, to start seeking that, so you can begin to trust him with this area of your life and ultimately grow your faith to believe in God for a future mate.

Seek Him First. As a woman of faith, the Scripture Matthew 6:33 has been quoted to me copious amounts of time. To the point where when I hear it, I almost tune out as I feel like I have heard every angle of this verse unpacked and/or preached. Looking at it with fresh eyes, I saw it in a new way. It states, *"But put God's Kingdom first. Do what he wants you to do. Then all those things will also be given to you."* (NIRV) Has someone ever said, in an effort to encourage you in your singleness, "keep your eyes fixed on God and focus on doing His work and then you will notice someone else doing the exact same work, and both of you will be running in the same direction. That's how you will meet your potential mate?" When I used to hear this, I thought *"I have been focused on doing God's work and His will for a long time, but I don't see anyone else running with me."*

If we go back to Matthew 6:33 and look at it, toward the end it says *"then all these things will be given to you."* Well right there, that should be enough to encourage and comfort us. We already know that God's Word is truth and His promises hold true. We also know that God does not lie and His very nature is promise keeper. So we can take heart in His Word that He promises to give us all these things. I believe marriage is one of those things that God wants to give us, but He needs us to put His Kingdom first and do what He says to do. So we can be confident that as we are putting God's Kingdom first, serving in His local church, doing works for His Kingdom, that He will give us a mate that is also doing the same thing. When we are putting God before our desire for marriage, and truly put him before it, that's when He blesses us, and that's when we begin to live out purity in our season of waiting.

Desire Vs. Need. I think it is important to talk about our need versus our desires, because many times we can get the two mixed up; especially in a season of waiting. We can start to convince ourselves, if we're not careful, that the thing we are waiting for is a need, when in actuality it is merely a desire. In this case that is marriage. The Oxford dictionary defines desire as a "a strong feeling of wanting to have something or wishing for something to happen."[xxv] The synonyms for "desire" are: "craving, pining, longing, ache, hunger, yearning."[xxvi]

It's interesting, because the Greek word for "seek" in Matthew 6:33 is *zéteó*, which literally means "desire." So God wants us to desire, yearn, long, crave, pine, ache and hunger first for the things of His Kingdom as opposed to earthly things. So as we learn to desire the right things, God will shift our perspective to those things we actually need.

The Merriam Webster dictionary defines a need as "a condition requiring supply or relief." That means that a need can be our basics: shelter, food, sleep, clothing, etc. These are things that every human being needs to survive. Notice how I didn't include a spouse? Meeting a man/woman you are going to spend the rest of your life with is not a necessity. It's simply a desire we have birthed by God himself. It's part of His plan for us and we need wait and trust that he has our best interest at heart. Can I just quickly address desires? It's okay to have them, after all we are only human. However, when those desires take the place of our relationship with God or become our sole purpose of focus, we have a problem.

One of the main desires that we as humans have and is always trying to attain is love. We want to be loved, because that is how God wired us. God is our father and He created us with a deep desire to be loved, so that He could love us. Let me repeat that again: God created us with a deep desire to be loved and he fulfills this desire by loving us first. Proverbs 27:20 states *"...the desires of men's hearts are insatiable."* (TPT) We will always have our own desires, but our aim should be to have Godly desires in our hearts and not our own human desires. Solomon says it here that human desires are never satisfied. How do we aim to have godly desires? David shows us how in Psalms 37:4: *"Delight yourself in the Lord, and he will give you the desires of your heart."* (ESV) As we spend time with our Father and get to know him, our desires are changed to godly desires and His promise is that He will give us the desires of our heart. That's why He loved us first. In Ephesians 3:18, Paul's prayers for the believers in Ephesus is that they *"may have the power to understand, as all God's people should, how wide, how long, how high and how deep his love is."* (NLT) God wants us to experience the full breadth of His love, so that our most prominent desire will be fulfilled.

If we aren't careful sometimes we can mistake our desires for need. Remember a need is something that when we get it, it sustains our life. However, a desire is merely a strong want, basically something we can continue to live without.

When you have been single for as long as I have, it's easier to fall into the trap of placing that desire as a priority in your life and therefore assuming it to be a need. Let me be straight with you, if you never meet that someone special, life will go on, you will still be alive. Unlike going without water for days on end, having the absence of an embrace will not kill you. I know sometimes it feels that if it doesn't happen that you are just going to die, but trust me that's not the case at all.

Be reassured that as you get filled with God's love and you get to know him, His desires become your desires. And as stated before God wants to give you your heart's desires. So be encouraged that if you have a close intimate relationship with God, it is likely that your desire is one that He placed there and He is going to fulfill it. Sorting out what our desires and needs are, is a great way to remain pure in our season of waiting.

Overcoming Discouragement. Discouragement is a word that most people including me try to avoid. We bury ourselves in work, church, friendships, family, exercise, etc. So why do we avoid this word? If you're anything like me, admitting you're discouraged makes you admit that you have become impatient, or lost hope in your situation.

The dictionary defines discouragement as "a loss of confidence or enthusiasm; dispiritedness." [xxvii] Basically discouragement is the loss of hope. No wonder we don't want to admit that we have lost our confidence and enthusiasm; it's just plain sad.

A while ago, I decided to take the plunge into the cyberspace world of online dating. I asked around discreetly, because at the time I didn't want anyone knowing that I was actually trying to date online. So I asked others about the best sites and prayed about it, just to make sure I was on the right track.

I signed up for three different sites so as to diversify my options. I was about two months into it and I hadn't had a date, let alone a decent conversation with any man. That excited anticipation and hope that once was, was slowly starting to fade as no prospects were surfacing. This was not without effort on my behalf. I winked, smiled and nudged my way through profiles. There were some conversations, but none of them lead to anything. So I gave up. I hadn't met anyone and I started to wonder if I was ever meant to be trying to date online in the first place. I started to question: "Am I not attractive enough to men? Where is the peace I once had about this? Why is this leading to nowhere when I thought God was encouraging me to go this way?" All these thoughts swirled around in my head and this great exciting experience quickly turned into a task on my to do list. I felt more like I was shopping for a husband and less diversifying my options, looking at the most viable options daily, what suited me the best. I didn't feel that God was in it at all anymore. So I decided to come off of online dating for good.

Sometime later the big 'D' word was beginning to loom over me so I threw myself into fasting and prayer, serving at my church, and going out with friends. Let's face it, it was all a distraction for how I was really feeling. That went on for about two more months, and then I finally broke down and admitted that I was very discouraged about my current marital status. I mean I had long let go of my plan to be married and with child by the age of 24, as I had just turned 34. That plan was clearly not going to happen.

I trusted God and knew that He was my Provider, but somewhere in the midst of me turning 34, having just ended my failed online experience and about to attend a wedding of my friends who were both 24, I just lost hope. To be honest, the next few months found me teetering in and out of discouragement.

～～～

Now I know this all sounds depressing, and I swear it gets better, this is just the beginning of my story and it isn't how it ends. God promises that *"the end of a matter is better than the beginning."* (Ecclesiastes 7:8, NIV) Let me give you hope if you too are feeling discouraged in this area or any area of your life. Like God promises the Israelites many times when they are discouraged, He will give them hope. Job 29:24 states *"when they were discouraged, I smiled at them. My look of approval was precious to them."* (NLT) God's promise for us is that He will encourage us when we are feeling discouraged. Job states that He smiles at us. One of the ways that God smiles at us, I believe, is through our daily blessings. Those little moments when a friend surprise visits you, you receive a compliment, when money appears out of nowhere, where God's love floods your heart or peace overwhelms your spirit. I want to encourage you to slow down today and notice all the ways in which God is smiling at you, encouraging you out of your season discouragement. As we learn to keep our eyes on God's little blessings in our lives, we can overcome discouragement and remain pure in our season of waiting.

His promise. God's promise for us is encouragement. His Word says that He will encourage those who are discouraged. So we can be certain that if God promises something that we can trust and hope that it will happen. We already know that God is not man that He should lie, so what He says He will do. He is our ultimate promise keeper; that's who He is, His character. If God has promised you a marriage and a family, be sure, confident, and hopeful that it will happen.

In the meantime while waiting for the fulfillment of our promise, we have to come to terms with patience. Patience is the ability to wait on/for the promises of God to come to pass in our lives. If we don't learn how to wait on God, then we will never receive His peace, love and hope while we wait. God wants us to have an abundant life, even in the midst of our waiting.

Remember I mentioned that discouragement is the lack of hope? Well the opposite of that is the abundance of hope. Solomon puts it well in Proverbs 13:12: *"It is sad not to get what you hope for. But wishes that come true are like eating fruit from the tree of life."* (NCV) We already know that God wants to give us our hearts' desires, but he also wants to change our desires before He gives us the desires of our heart.

With that said, He also knows that there will be things we want in life that we may never get because that's not what God wants for us. Of course, that will make us sad, but the second part of that verse promises us that our wishes (not all) can come true.

A wish is defined as something we want- a desire. It is so sweet when our wants/desires line up with God's and He gives us that desire. Solomon assimilates it to eating fruit from the tree of life. The tree of life was first mentioned in Genesis, where it states that it was planted in the middle of Garden of Eden just beside the tree of knowledge of good and evil. This tree had to have been a very important tree for it to be planted in the middle of the garden. And if its anything like the tree of the knowledge of good and evil, the fruit must be very tasty.

So Solomon says that desires that are fulfilled are like eating fruit from the tree of life. God wants us to experience our hearts' desires coming to pass, because He knows what it feels like. So if your heart's desire is like mine, to get married and have children, then pray about it. Ask God to confirm that the desire is from him, and then wait on him to deliver that promise. We already know that when it is fulfilled it will taste so sweet to our souls. Sometimes I think of God sitting up there in heaven being able to see the end, just giddy with anticipation of what's to come for us, His children. Let me leave you with this: *"Why am I discouraged? Why is my heart so sad? I will put my hope in God! I will praise him again- my Saviour."* (Psalm 42:5, NLT) Lay all your cards on the table before God and allow him to work in your heart the encouragement he has for you. If marriage is in your heart, have hope in God for that. I will be waiting right alongside of you.

Let's pick up in my story from when I first started writing this book. I was 32 and I remember that God challenged me on the motives of my heart in wanting to get married. Great stuff! As I write today, I am still single. I don't claim to be the expert on this subject, but I would love to share my experiences with you about waiting in the hope you won't make the same mistakes I did, and be able to remain pure in our waiting period:

If we aren't careful we could make the actual waiting process an idol in our lives. Feelings are very deceptive; we should never let them help us decide. God has rest for us in the waiting period, as we learn to trust in him.

God comes first. Let's take the first item. God should always be number one in our lives. God was the one who gave us the desires in our heart. He knows what we want, but He also knows what we need. God typically gives us what we *need* before he gives us what we *want*. Sometimes He has to change our character before He blesses us with what we want so that we can fully enjoy His blessing. Proverbs 10:22 states that *"The blessing of the Lord makes a person rich, and he adds no sorrow with it."* (NLT) So God wants to bless us richly, but He also wants us to enjoy it. He doesn't want us worrying if it's going to be taken away, or constantly dealing with insecurities. No, He wants us to be healthy and whole so that we can really enjoy that thing He has blessed us with. In this case, it's our marriages- He wants us to truly enjoy that season of our lives.

Please know that I am not saying that we are never going to go through challenges in our marriages, but even in the presence of them we are going to enjoy the ride. Don't we serve an awesome God? Not only does He have good things to us, but He wants us to enjoy those blessings.

a) *Daily Bible reading.* So how do we make God number one in our lives? Well these are a couple staples that I do in my life to make sure God is always first. Firstly, I read my Bible daily. Like I said before, God's Word is alive and if we are reading it daily, He can begin to speak a myriad of things to encourage us in this season.

b) *Daily Devotionals.* I have devotional time with God daily. Now that can look very different for each individual. For me it consists of Bible reading, worship, prayer and sometimes journaling depending on how much time I have. I try to journal at least once a week. A mentor of mine always says "If you're not meeting with God every day, you are trying to be a Christian without Christ." (Brenda Abram-Nakamura, founder and creator of Single to Married, God's Way) So it's important to have time set aside each day to spend with God.

c) *Daily prayer.* I pray every day. I know this was included in the second one, but the benefits of it is worth mentioning all on its own merit. God gave me a vision for my life back in 2013 that I would be a prayer warrior. At the end of 2012 I went on my very

PURIFY YOUR LIFE 83

first missions' trip to South Africa. At the end of the first day I was very discouraged. I wanted to pray for people, but I was scared to. I allowed fear to take over me. That night we got into groups and prayed with and for each other. I confessed that I was scared to pray with people, so they prayed over me for boldness when I pray. The rest of the trip I had come way out of my comfort zone and was praying for everyone I met! So much so that by the end of the trip people were calling me a prayer warrior. So God was giving me a vision to remind me of what He placed within me.

At the beginning of 2016, I challenged myself to up my prayer life. I wanted to start praying daily and be more consistent about it. I decided to keep a prayer journal and adopted the S.T.O.P. method for praying (Sorry, Thanks, Others, Petition). Prayer is merely conversation with God. It's also another way God speaks to us. How can God encourage us if in our time of waiting we aren't communicating with him? I challenge you if you aren't praying daily to start a prayer journal. It keeps you accountable and also helps you track answered prayers.

d) *Get planted.* I am planted in a local church. Part of God's master plan is the church- the local church to be exact. God made us for relationship with him and with each other. So that's why it's important to get into a local church. When I say I am planted, I mean I don't only attend church once a week. I take classes my church offers, I have made friends in my church, and I serve in my church. How else am I supposed to grow if I don't have godly friendships in my life? As the Bible says *"iron sharpens iron, so a friend sharpens a friend."* (Psalm 27:17, NLT) It's through relationships that we are able to truly develop the fruits of the

Holy Spirit: peace, joy, love, kindness, humility, patience, goodness, faithfulness and self-control. (Galatians 5:22-23, NLT)

By serving in my local church I have placed God first in my life. For those of you, like me, who have found your season of singleness to be a time of loneliness; serving in a local church is a great way to meet new people. When you are serving in your local church, your focus is on others and not on your own life. When serving, by nature we will end up feeling better about life, plus it's a great way to love on people. I have always believed the thing you want most, you should be willing to give away. So if you want to be loved, you should be loving others.

I will be praying for you as you aim to remain pure in your season of waiting, by putting God first, spend time with him, focusing on your blessing, putting your whole trust in God and clinging to His hope. Allow God to shape and mold you in the season.

CHAPTER 6: PURITY IN LEADERSHIP

At the end of 2016 I was placed in a leadership role within our church's Children's Ministry. I went from assisting the Children's pastor to becoming the ministry director and making decisions about the ministry. I remember being so excited and honoured that they chose me to be able to do what I do and that they believed in me that much. I learned very fast that leadership had nothing to do with the title I received. It was a lifestyle. We all have been called to be leaders in our lives. As Christians, we have been called to be in the world but not of the world. (John 17:14-19) God has given all of us a sphere of influence. How will you use your's? The dictionary defines leadership as: "the quality of character and personality giving a person the ability to gain the confidence of and lead others."[xxviii] That's all of us in our walks with God. We have been called to stand out and be set apart. (Leviticus 20:26)

It was in this season of my career that I learned all about purity in leadership; having the right attitude and perspective and being confident that you have been equipped and that God is with you. You see, a higher position meant greater responsibility. Joshua was called to stand out. When God called him to be a leader to the Israelites he called him to stand out. God had already equipped him, but told him some tips that would help him remain pure in this season: meditating on His Word day and night, keeping God first in everything, trust in God, and tapping into the strength and courage which God had already given him. (Joshua 1)

When I first came to God, I remember asking what my purpose was in this new life. As I spent time with him (through prayer, worship, and devotional time) He told me I would work in Children's ministry, and more specifically that I would be an Administrator for the ministry. That's one of those dreams, you end up putting on the shelf, because you hope one day it would happen, but ultimately God is in control.

Here I am today; I am my church's Children's Ministry Administrator. The specific Word God spoke to me has come to pass in my life. Now I don't know about you, but that was the first time God had spoken a really big dream to me and it actually happened. Albeit, it was five and half years later, but it came to pass! I was ecstatic!

Fast forward six months later after I started my new position as Children ministry director, and that excitement I once had all but disappeared. The job consisted of about 85-90% of administrative work and the rest creative work. As much as I am gifted in administration I do enjoy and get passionate about the creative aspects of my job more. So it was a bit of a struggle for me. As well, shortly after I started the job my finances became tight. That coupled with my surprising apathy for this new position made me start questioning whether or not I was called to work for the church. I struggled for the next six months, seeking God through it all. All the while I kept hearing from the Lord that I should remain faithful.

I was in a mentoring session with our lead pastor's wife, and the last thing she said to us was how she and her husband remained faithful and humbled themselves by serving where they were placed in the church and she believed that is why they are lead pastors over our church today. That weekend, our pastor shared a message on how to build a firm foundation in our lives. One of the ways was remaining faithful.

WHAT I LEARNED

In the short time I have had this role, I learned a few key things about what purity in leadership looks like:

It's not always going to be glamorous, exciting or fun! I don't say this to deter you from ever desiring a leadership position. However, when I first came into this position I had on rose-colored glasses. I thought that since it was my "dream" job that it was going to be the most amazing job ever. I would have fun every day, cast vision often with our Children's Pastor and it was going to be a big party.

Let me say that yes, there are moments where all that happens. On the flip side, the job is hard work. 85% of my job is spent doing administration for the ministry, thinking through processes and procedures, setting up schedules, writing and organizing curriculum, organizing other various parts of the ministry, sending out correspondence, overseeing recruitment and application to our ministry and so forth. Then there is the cleaning, going through our children's classrooms on a regular basis to make sure everything is in order. My job description is not just Director, but cleaner, folder, planner, printer, sorter, typist, etc. There are many different hats that I put on for this role.

This year I learned about effective communication with volunteers. I learned about how to roll out a new process and how long that takes. I learned about the patience that is required to work out all the kinks. I learned about staying on top of things to make sure things are running smoothly all the time.

When I think about the last 24 months, the words "glamorous," "exciting," or "fun" did not come up as often. Yes, I did have fun, but I also worked very hard. True ministry is gritty and dirty and rough. You need to have an attitude of just rolling up your sleeves and getting in there. In those moments where my job wasn't as glamorous I had to really dig deep and remember why I wanted the job in the first place. I had to go back to my why.

I really want to encourage you, if you believe you are on the path where God has called you and it didn't turn out the way you thought it would, go back to your why. Why did you want to take that path; what was your motivation? I find that when you keep the bigger picture in front of you all the time, it makes those seasons of struggles worth it- knowing that there is light at the end of the tunnel.

Become and stay humble. Over the last year this was a hard lesson for me to learn. I went through a season where I just felt ignored, looked over and underappreciated. I spent my time making our volunteers and our ministry look good. "But what about me?" I would say. I was working so hard and I felt like no one noticed me.

In this season all I could think of was what one of pastors had always said. He measured success by how well the others did on the team and if he wasn't noticed behind the scenes that was his aim. He explained that our heart shouldn't be to be noticed for our work, but allow our work to get God noticed. 1 Corinthians 10:31 states *"whatever you do, do it all for the glory of God."* (NLT) Our aim in everything we do, including leading a team/ministry/family should be to bring glory to God. Whether it's in how we lead, or how we treat others. In this case, it's being and remaining humble.

I have to admit that was a hard concept for my mind to wrap around in this season. I was just given a new position of leadership that allowed me more responsibility, more hours of work, more pay. And now you wanted me to just sit in the background, while everyone got the glory for all my hard work? Hey, don't judge me! I'm not perfect. This was truly my struggle. Even as I type this, I am thoroughly ashamed of my rotten attitude.

God was humbling me. God had to teach me that my promotion was not about me, but others. When I was constantly overlooked time and time again, I felt so dejected. But I felt God pushing me to not give up! (Galatians 6:9) Most of the time God is not interested in our circumstances, but in our character development. God has a plan for our lives and He needs to shape us and mold us through our circumstances in order to make us into someone He can use. (2 Timothy 2:21)

In Matthew 23:12 Jesus says, *"Whoever exalts himself will be humbled, and he who humbles himself will be exalted."* (NKJV) God had to remove pride from me so He used and is still using this job to humble me. Each day, God is teaching me that He gave me this position in order to glorify him. My success since I started this job was in the moments that allowed God to get the glory- I decreased as He increased.

Remain faithful. There were many times when I just wanted to pack it in and find a new job. Now for some of you reading this who know me, you may be surprised. I remember just before I was offered this new role, I was looking for other jobs. I was about to apply for a job with another company in my city. It was my dream job, something I have always wanted to do. I was going to apply that evening as the application was due. That same day my boss came up to me and showed me my new job description. Get this, my new job description included everything that this other job did; the job I was going to apply for. I remember thinking from that point on that quitting my job was no longer on the table. I resolved that if God had called me to this job, that I was going to stay. So I removed the thought from my mind.

Six months into the job and in the midst of my boredom, financial hardship, I was tempted again to leave my job. But everything inside of me continued to listen to that still small voice that told me to remain faithful. The six months that proceeded had my emotions going like a roller coaster. My heart was torn between thoughts of "I can't do this anymore," to "God, I know you called me to this so why do I feel this way?"

I feel like this is all part of taking on new territory, that when it gets really difficult you may feel like you just want to give up, turn around and run away. But there is something to be said for remaining faithful. Solomon states *"a faithful person will be richly blessed."* (Proverbs 28:20, NIRV) When we remain faithful God will not only bless us, but richly bless us. In Luke Jesus talks about how when we are faithful with little we will be faithful with much (Luke 16:10). So through the lack or suffering we are feeling now, Jesus urges us to be faithful because God will then know that we can be trusted with more than what we are entrusted with today. So if you are certain God called you to where you are right now, and you have thoughts like "I can't do this," or "I just need to leave here", let me encourage you to remain faithful. You will be glad you did; the reward is worth it!

Serve others. There is one Scripture that sums it all up quite nicely of how we are supposed to lead. The mother of Zebedee's sons just asked Jesus if her sons can sit beside him on the throne in heaven. In response to her request Jesus says this in Matthew 20: 24-28:

"The other ten disciples heard about this. They became angry at the two brothers. Jesus called them together. He said, "You know about the rulers of the Gentiles. They hold power over their people. Their high officials order them around. Don't be like that. Instead, anyone who wants to be important among you must be your servant. And anyone who wants to be first must be your slave. Be like the Son of Man. He did not come to be served. Instead, he came to serve others. He came to give his life as the price for setting many people free." (NIRV- emphasis added)

Lead from a place of servitude. What are you willing to do for others? I believe the amount you are willing to do to serve others is in direct correlation to the success you will have in leadership. Jesus is our perfect example. Although he was the Son of God, he emptied himself, gave up His heavenly power, to become a human and ultimately give up His earthly body for all of us. Jesus healed, delivered, preached and prayed for many people. He was constantly serving others. I want to encourage you to truly look at your leadership role, and think about what you are doing to serve others on a daily basis?

Be teachable and open to correction. This last one is one of the most important for being in a role of leadership. How can you prepare yourself to receive more when you are stuck where you are? In order to prepare for more, you need to grow. You grow by learning. You learn by being taught and corrected.

I remember when I first stepped into my new role at the church. I would send out an email, or make a decision about a process, and then an email would come in with the words "Some feedback" in the subject line. I swallowed that huge lump in my throat and faced the email. I have a hard time with criticism- constructive criticism that is. Sometimes I feel like I don't have any blind spots, until I spend time in prayer and devotion with God, and He would gently gives me "some feedback" about my heart.

When I first started to receive those emails, my first response was fight. I felt like I had to explain and defend my choices and ideas. It wasn't an easy process for me; receiving feedback. But as I received more and more of it over time, it did get a bit easier. Something began to happen to me. As I spent time with God He began to show me that constructive criticism was all about the growth process. He begins to answer my prayer for extended grace in order for me receive feedback. At that same time God has me on a journey of security. He was making me secure in who I was and who He created me to be. It's a bit easier to receive criticism once you know who you are and secure in that.

I started accepting all of me, even those "bad" areas (weaknesses). I knew that God loved me no matter what, even when I made a mistake. I even started to laugh at my mistakes, and truly thanked others for taking the time to give me some feedback. I wouldn't say that I am pro at receiving feedback, but now it doesn't wreck me like it used to.

Feedback is an essential part for our growth. And being able to receive correction is important to our growth. Yes, my mistakes were highlighted, but they didn't define me. Who I am had nothing to do with the mistakes I had made. They were two completely different things.

Solomon was wise. I mean that's what he asked for when God asked him what he wanted out of anything in the world. Solomon states in Proverbs: *"Let wise people listen and add to what they have learned. Let those who understand what is right get guidance."* (Proverbs 1:5, NIRV) He stressed the importance of learning- adding to what you have already learned. Throughout the Proverbs, Solomon states over and over that we should seek wisdom. That takes having a teachable heart, first to admit that you don't know everything, and second, to admit that you want to learn more.

As a leader it so important to have a teachable spirit. Those that you lead will only grow as much you are willing to grow. The more you grow the more you can serve them and feed them.

The most important thing that you should remember is that promotion comes from God, not you. So stop striving, and surrender it all to God. When you lay it at His feet is when you can truly lead from a place of purity. And that is beautiful purity in leadership right there.

CONCLUSION

At the beginning of the book I defined purity as: *the process of removing impurity (in thoughts, words and actions) from your life.* I took it one step further and looked at Galatians 5. It was all about how we should aim to live according to the Spirit and not our sinful nature. This allows us to rid ourselves of the sin that so easily entangles us. I want to conclude this book by looking at Romans 6:12-14:

"That means you must not give sin a vote in the way you conduct your lives. Don't give it the time of day. Don't even run little errands that are connected with that old way of life. Throw yourselves wholeheartedly and full-time—remember, you've been raised from the dead! —into God's way of doing things. Sin can't tell you how to live. After all, you're not living under that old tyranny any longer. You're living in the freedom of God." (MSG)

As Christian's we have been called into the light. The sin we used to live in no longer claims our souls, but we have been given new lives through the Holy Spirit who lives on the inside of us. Paul says it plainly in verse 12 that we should not "run little errands that are connected with that old way of life." Think about it this way, if the devil was on the earth today as a living person and he came up to you and asked you to go get him a coffee, knowing who he was, would you go? Paul is saying here don't give in to sin in the slightest; don't even run those little errands on its behalf in our lives. Sin is meant to sully our lives and remove the purity that we are aiming to achieve, which God calls us to live out in every area of our lives:

Finances. When it comes to managing our finances, we need to keep God at the centre of it. Verse 12 says that we must not give sin a vote in the way we conduct our lives. This means that jealousy, greed, covetousness and selfishness should have nothing do with the way we steward our finances. Our aim should be to bring glory to God in the way we steward our finances. Remember as we aim to be content with what we have and trust God to provide for our every need (Philippians 4:19), we will continue to live out purity in our finances.

Emotions. Whether we are experiencing anger, offence, doubt or fear we must always remember that God has given us a Spirit of self-control. We have a choice of whether or not we will react negatively to those emotions. Verse 13 states that we must throw ourselves *"wholeheartedly and full-time...into God's way of doing things."* God calls us to not live by our feelings- carnal nature but by the spirit who lives on the inside of us; helping us throw ourselves into God's way of doing things. Purity in emotions is even in the face of negative emotions, deciding to live by God's ways: love, peace, self control and forgiveness. By choosing to live this way it will ensure that we are living out purity in this area of our lives.

Relationships. This verse sums up what purity in relationships should be: *"Love your neighbour as yourself."* (Matthew 22:39, NLT) If we strive to put others before us and serve those in our lives than we will have success in our relationships. A great question to always ask yourself is "Am I being a good_____?" (sibling/friend/child/parent/coworker. You fill in the blank.) What do you do on a regular basis for each relationship in your life? Relationships are hard work and they take effort to make them successful. Remember how Romans 6:12 says that we are to not run little errands for sin- that old way of life? That means when someone close to you hurts you, forgive them and learn to love despite their actions. We are imperfect beings and we are all bound to hurt each other. The key to successful relationships is extending grace, learning to forgive and most importantly always loving them.

Mind. The greatest battle we face on a daily basis is one that happens where no one can see and that is in the mind. The last part of verse 14 reminds us that: *"You're living in the freedom of God."* Paul wants us to remember that we have already been given the freedom in those areas in which struggle, whether that be lustful or negative thoughts. We must always remember the freedom we were given on the cross. His blood was shed in order for us to experience victory over our old ways of thinking. We can operate in the mindset of battlefield versus a mine field of the mind. We have been given weapons to use on the battlefield.

Waiting. Waiting is something that all of us have in common no matter what season of life we are in. The key to keeping ourselves pure in any season of waiting is to move "our focus from the object of our wait to the Person of our faith."[xxix] Romans 6:13 states: *"Throw yourselves...full-time...—into God's way of doing things."* (MSG) When you find yourself in a season of waiting there are things that you could be doing in order to let the time pass by. As I discussed in the chapter, waiting is not passive, it requires action. If you're single and waiting for your spouse, what are you doing now to better yourself before you get married? Are you going after the purpose of God for your life? Do you even know what that purpose is? My suggestion to you is pray to God and ask what you should be throwing yourselves into full time as you wait. There is a season for everything in our lives (Ecclesiastes 3:1) and the waiting period is a time to get involved in God's work. Trust me, that waiting period won't seem so long when you are busy doing God's work.

Leadership. True leadership consists of serving others over yourself. Purity in leadership takes the shape of humility, servitude, commitment, perseverance, strength and integrity. In order for us to truly be successful in leadership we need to figure out what those around us need and work towards giving them that. Verse 13 states: *"-remember, you've been raised from the dead!"* We need to remember that Christ died for us to give us the Holy Spirit which is a Spirit of power. We need to tap into the power the Holy Spirit gives us in order to lead in purity. It's only through the Holy Spirit that we will manifest what pure leadership is meant to look like. Remember that *"when someone has been entrusted with much, even more will be required."* (Luke 12:48, NLT). That means as leaders more is required from us; more self-control, more servitude, more humility, more perseverance, more right living, etc. That's why we need to tap into the endless power of Holy Spirit living on the inside of us in order to maintain purity as leaders.

At the end of the day purity is a journey, it is not perfection. What you read in these pages are meant to be guidelines of what to attain to, not what should be achieved now. We are running a marathon not a sprint. My suggestion to you is take a chapter a month and challenge yourself in one aspect of that chapter to work on in your life. Don't be so hard on yourself if you're not where you want to be. God sees your heart and your intention to want to be become pure. He will help you along the way. I hope this book has blessed you as much as it has blessed me to write it. I will be praying for each and every one of you reading my book. You got this!

EPILOGUE

Anchors, Butterflies and Crosses

Anchors. You are probably wondering what anchors, butterflies or crosses have to do with purity. This is my story filled with hope, promises and joy amidst the struggles and pain. This is my journey to purity.

It was the end of the 2013 when I was in the middle of the greatest season of hope: Christmas. But I struggled to hold on to the hope that was already inside of me. I was convinced that I had no hope. I was living with my parents at the time, and saying that living with them was a struggle is an understatement. There was constant fighting and no peace. I was in the middle of completing our church's internship and working part time. So the funds to move out were just not there. I felt stuck.

We had a guest speaker at our church one weekend and he was speaking about hope. I remember feeling guilty thinking that as a woman of faith I should have had hope. He reminded me that we have this hope that lives on the inside of us. A living hope.

As I was praying one night, a picture of an anchor popped into my head and I was lead to read Hebrews 6:19 which states *"This hope is like an anchor for us. It is strong and sure and keeps us safe."* (ERV) Anchors were created to hold something still, such as a boat that naturally tends to float away with the waves. That's what God's hope does for us; it keeps us grounded in His love and peace no matter what situation we are going through.

I believe that was God giving me renewed strength and a different outlook on the situation with my family. He removed the fear and doubt, and purified my heart to have hope again in my situation but not just any hope, a hope that kept me grounded in him, a hope that allowed me to hope for change in my situation despite how it looked.

Butterflies. Going into a new year that feeling of being stuck was very prevalent within me. I remember thinking that I was in a job I didn't quite like, and still living at home with my parents. I felt like I was not in control of my life, that my situation was never going to change. Have you ever felt like that? Like you can't seem to see a way out of your current situation?

That night I prayed to God, and a picture of a butterfly popped into my head. I connected to that picture of a butterfly. It got me excited about the notion of the freedom I was going to attain. Butterflies go through a process of metamorphosis, which means that they change their state/shape. I believe that 2014 was the beginning of my metamorphosis.

Remember that feeling of being stuck? Well, by April of that year I had finished the internship, left my job, went on a mission trip, paid off my internship, and got a new job working for the church. Oh and I also moved out of my parents' house. My life was starting to change its state and shape right before my eyes. This was not the end of my metamorphosis.

The middle phase of change in the life of a caterpillar to butterfly is called the chrysalis or pupa. The word chrysalis means "a preparatory or transitional state."[xxx] The caterpillar is encased in leaves and hidden from the world. During this phase they shed the parts of them that they no longer need, and start growing the parts they do need. This is all done in seclusion.

During this phase of our lives, it can be hard. We can easily feel like we have been forgotten and overlooked. This state of preparation is key to us becoming butterflies. It is through this phase of my life that I grew in faith, in security in who I truly am and in sincere love for people. During this phase I saw great freedom take place in my life from lust, negative thoughts, self-doubt, etc. This was a season of true purification in my life. As I come to the end of my chrysalis season I am thankful for all the lessons learned and how my feet are now secure. Psalm 18:33 states "He makes my feet like *[a] hinds' feet [able to stand firmly and tread safely on paths of testing and trouble]; He sets me [securely] upon my high places."* (AMP) God was teaching me to stand securely on my high places. I am confident in knowing that my season of flying is coming soon which would have only happened by going through the purified state of chrysalis. I can't wait to embrace it.

Crosses. During my chrysalis season, the symbol of the cross was so important. Words like: "You're not good enough," "your mouth is going to get you into trouble," "you're not talented," "why bother dreaming," "you're not ready for that," etc. were spoken over me. So much so that I started to believe those words about myself. Even after God revealed the truth that: I am more than enough, I am loved, I am chosen, I am called, I am free, I am redeemed, I am a daughter of the Most High King, etc. (Look at the image called "Who I Am in Christ" in the Appendix B) to me I still had a hard time dropping the labels that were cast over me. I knew who I was and the freedom I had gained, but I struggled to hold onto that truth.

The Cross symbolizes ultimate freedom. If you are unfamiliar with the story of Jesus, He is the Son of God that was born to save you and me. He died a horrible death on the cross so that through the shedding of His blood we would be free from sin once and for all.

Free from all sin you ask? How can that be? Because He lives today those who believe in him also live. He died to break the power of sin over all of us, past, present and future sins, once and for all. He died to give us freedom from death. That's right, if you believe in Jesus and that He died on a cross for your sins, you are also free from eternal death.

The blood of Jesus purified us who believe from every sin we committed or will commit. In the Bible it talks about a time of ritual sacrifices (blood shed) that were made to atone for the sins of man. Well just think of Jesus as the ultimate shedding of blood for our sins. There is no sin you commit that could ever keep you in bondage. You have been set free once and for all!

I did an exercise so that I could remember the power of the Cross and what it meant to me. I made a picture of a cross and taped it to the back of my book shelf and then wrote down all my past sins that I believed Jesus had set me free from on individual post it notes. I then posted each sin on top of the cross to represent my sins being nailed to the cross one by one.

Romans 8:1 states *"So now there is no condemnation for those who belong to Christ Jesus."* (NLT) When you belong to Jesus, believe in him, you are free from being condemned for any sins you committed in the past or will commit in the future. Your sin is gone, and Jesus paid the price once and for all.

When you give your life to Jesus and believe that He died on a cross to save you from your sins, your *"old life is gone, and a new life has begun."* (2 Corinthians 5:17, NLT) Another version says *"Old things have passed way, behold, all things have become new."* (2 Corinthians 5:17, NKJV) All your old sins have been nailed to the cross once and for all- you have been set free from them. Therefore, you have now been given the power to overcome those old sins once and for all. When they try to come creeping back in, remember that you are a new creation and that started from the time you said yes to Jesus. Embrace the newness of your life as God shapes and molds you into a better version of yourself. Just watch how the cross will transform your life as His hope anchors your soul so that you can fly into the freedom He has for you like a butterfly- the way you were truly meant to be. This, my friends, is what living a life of purity is all about. Remember we are on a journey to fulfill our God-given purposes. So, let us aim, but keeping our lives pure, to be *"used for every good work"* (2 Timothy 2:21) by the Master- God himself.

~~~

If you have never accepted a life with Jesus and would like to, turn to the next page.

APPENDIX A

The Sinners Prayer

Dear God,
I need you,
I am humbly calling out to you,
I'm tired of doing things my way,
I invite you into my life to be
My Lord and Saviour,
Fill the emptiness in me with your
Holy Spirit and make me whole.
Lord, help me to love you,
Help me to live for you,
Help me to understand your grace
Your mercy, and your peace.
In Jesus' name,
Amen

APPENDIX B

Who I am in Christ

I am a new creation in Christ! - 2 Corinthians 5:17
I am chosen. I am holy. - 1 Peter 2:9
I am God's very own possession. - Galatians 2:20
I am God's beloved. - John 15:15
I am a friend of God. - John 1:12
I am an heir to God's glory. - Romans 8:17
I am a citizen of heaven. - Philippians 3:20
God gave his one and only son for me. God loves me so much. - John 3:16
I am the temple of God. - 1 Corinthians 3:16
I am more than a conqueror. - Romans 8:37
I am fearfully and wonderfully made. God knew me before I was born. He knit me together in my mother's womb. - Psalm 139:13-16
God has a plan for my life. - Jeremiah 29:11
I am created in God's image. - Genesis 1:27
I am chosen by God. I was adopted into God's family. - Ephesians 1:4-5
I am saved by God. God has identified me as his own. God wants to give me an inheritance. - Ephesians 1:13-14
The hairs on my head are counted. I am valuable to God. - Luke 12:7
I am God's masterpiece. - Ephesians 2:10
I am a member of God's family. - Ephesians 2:19

E G W MINISTRIES

RESOURCES

Great resources I mentioned in my book:

1. *Wait and See* by Wendy Pope

2. *Boundaries* by Dr.'s Henry Cloud and John Townsend

3. *Battlefield of the Mind* by Joyce Meyers

4. *Dating Manifesto* by Lisa Anderson

5. Single to Married God's Way: https://www.singletomarriedgodsway.com/

6. Get One Word: http://getoneword.com/

7. *Honor's Reward* by Messenger International

8. Fasting: https://www.ihopkc.org/about/fasting-guidelines-and-information/

REFERENCES

[i] J.D. Douglas, N. Hillyer, F.F. Bruce, D. Guthrie, A.R. Millard, J.I. Packer, and D.J. Wiseman. *The New Bible Dictionary, Second Edition* (Illinois: Intervarsity Press, 1994), 1002.

[ii] Douglas et al. *The New Bible Dictionary Second Edition*, 1002.

[iii] "Oxford Living Dictionaries." Oxford University Press. Last modified: 2018. https://en.oxforddictionaries.com/definition/purity.

[iv] NAS Exhaustive Concordance of the Bible with Hebrew-Aramaic and Greek Dictionaries. (1998: The Lockman Foundation) Bible Hub Greek dictionary online. *apotithémi*

[v] Dave Ramsey. *The Total Money Makeover: A Proven Plan for Financial Fitness*. (Nashville: Thomas Nelson Inc., 2007)

[vi] "Oxford Living Dictionaries." Oxford University Press. Last modified: 2018. https://en.oxforddictionaries.com/definition/steward.

[vii] "What does it mean to repent?" The Church of Jesus Christ of Latter Day Saints. Last Modified: September 2016. https://www.lds.org/youth/learn/ap/atonement/repent?lang=eng&_r=1.

[viii] "Bible Hub: Search, Read, Study the Bible in Many Lanugages." Bible Hub. Last modified: 2018. http://biblehub.com/greek/5483.htm

[ix] "Merriam Webster Dictionaries." Merriam Webster Inc. Last modified: 2018. https://www.merriam-webster.com/dictionary/offend.

[x] "Bible Study Tools." Salem Web Network. Last modified: 2018. http://www.biblestudytools.com/lexicons/greek/nas/proskomma.html.

[xi] "Merriam Webster Dictionaries." Merriam Webster Inc. Last modified: 2018. https://www.merriam-webster.com/dictionary/doubt.

[xii] Beth Moore. *Praying the Word of God*. (Nashville: B & H Publishing Group, 2009),19-32.

[xiii] "Merriam Webster Dictionaries." Merriam Webster Inc. Last modified: 2018. https://www.merriam-webster.com/dictionary/fear.
[xiv] "Merriam Webster Dictionaries." Merriam Webster Inc. Last modified: 2018. https://www.merriam-webster.com/thesaurus/banish.
[xv] Stumvoll, Abi. "Who Do You Want To Attract // Day 8 // Abi Stumvoll." *YouTube*, Moral Revolution, 30 June 2018, youtu.be/at2BNbQrt_Q.
[xvi] "Learner's Dictionary." Merriam-Webster Inc. Last modified: 2018. http://www.learnersdictionary.com/definition/authority.
[xvii] "Messenger International." Messenger International, Inc. Last modified: 2018. https://store.messengerinternational.org/products/honor-s-reward-curriculum-video-download.
[xviii] "Cambridge Dictionary." Cambridge University Press. Last modified: 2018. https://dictionary.cambridge.org/dictionary/english/lust.
[xix] "Bible Study Tools." Salem Web Network. Last modified: 2018. http://www.biblestudytools.com/dictionary/lust/.
[xx] "Oxford Living Dictionaries." Oxford University Press. Last modified: 2018. https://en.oxforddictionaries.com/definition/emotion.
[xxi] "Bible Hub: Search, Read, Study the Bible in Many Lanugages." Bible Hub. Last modified: 2018. http://biblehub.com/greek/3794.htm.
[xxii] Hanks, Patrick, et al. *Oxford Dictionary of English*. Oxford University Press, 2010.
[xxiii] "New York Review Books." New York Review Books. Last modified: 2018. https://www.nyrb.com/products/the-chrysalids.
[xxiv] "Your Dictionary." LoveToKnow, Corp. Last modified: 2018. http://examples.yourdictionary.com/negative-thinking-examples.html.
[xxv] "Oxford Living Dictionaries." Oxford University Press. Last modified: 2018. https://en.oxforddictionaries.com/definition/desire.
[xxvi] "Oxford Living Dictionaries." Oxford University Press. Last modified: 2018. https://en.oxforddictionaries.com/thesaurus/desire.
[xxvii] "Oxford Living Dictionaries." Oxford University Press. Last modified: 2018. https://en.oxforddictionaries.com/definition/discouragement.

[xxviii] "The Free Dictionary." The Farlex Inc. Last modified: 2018. https://www.thefreedictionary.com/Leadership.

[xxix] Pope, Wendy. *Wait and See*. Colorado: David C Cook, 2016. pgs. 106-7.

[xxx] "Google Search Dictionary." Google. Last modified: 2018. https://www.google.com/search?rlz=1C5CHFA_enCA782CA783&q=Dictionary#dobs=chrysalis.

Made in the USA
Monee, IL
20 December 2021